Mathematics in the K–8 Classroom and Library

Mathematics in the K–8 Classroom and Library

Sueanne McKinney and KaaVonia Hinton

AN IMPRINT OF ABC-CLIO, LLC
Santa Barbara, California • Denver, Colorado • Oxford, England

Copyright 2010 by ABC-CLIO, LLC

All rights reserved. No part of this publication may be reproduced, stored in a retrieval system, or transmitted, in any form or by any means, electronic, mechanical, photocopying, recording, or otherwise, except for the inclusion of brief quotations in a review, without prior permission in writing from the publisher.

Library of Congress Cataloging-in-Publication Data
McKinney, Sueanne.
  Mathematics in the K–8 classroom and library / Sueanne McKinney and KaaVonia Hinton.
    p. cm.
  Includes index.
    ISBN 978-1-58683-522-4 (alk. paper) — ISBN 978-1-58683-523-1 (ebook)
  1. Literature in mathematics education. 2. Mathematics—Study and teaching (Elementary) I. Hinton, KaaVonia, 1973– II. Title.
    QA19.L58M35 2010
    372.7—dc22   2010007011

ISBN: 978-1-58683-522-4
EISBN: 978-1-58683-523-1

14 13 12 11 10   1 2 3 4 5

This book is also available on the World Wide Web as an eBook.
Visit www.abc-clio.com for details.

Linworth
An Imprint of ABC-CLIO, LLC

ABC-CLIO, LLC
130 Cremona Drive, P.O. Box 1911
Santa Barbara, California 93116-1911

This book is printed on acid-free paper ∞

Manufactured in the United States of America

In memory of my parents, Joseph and Betty Ann McKinney.
—Sueanne E. McKinney

In memory of my father, Erskine H. Lawrence.
—KaaVonia Hinton

Contents

Figures xiii
About the Authors xv
Introduction xvii

CHAPTER 1: Using Literature in the Mathematics Classroom and Library 1
Linking Mathematics and Literature 2
Evaluating Mathematical Literature Selections 2
Advantages of Linking Mathematics and Literature 2
Linking Mathematics with Writing 5
Works Cited 5
Children's Books Cited 7

CHAPTER 2: Collaborating with Mathematics Teachers 9
To Mathematics Teachers 10
To Librarians 10
Works Cited 12

CHAPTER 3: Number and Operations 15
Number and Operations Expectations 16
Counting 16
Using Mathematics Literature 16
    A Creepy Countdown 16
    Fish Eyes: A Book You Can Count On 17
    One Less Fish 17
    The M&M's Count to One Hundred Book 17
    Dreaming: A Countdown to Sleep 17
    Suggestions for Classroom Use 17
        Journaling 18
Addition and Subtraction 18
    How the Second Grade Got $8,205.50 to Visit the Statue of Liberty .. 19
    Suggestions for Classroom Use 19
        Journaling 21
    The Grapes of Math 21
    Suggestions for Classroom Use 21
        Journaling 22
    How Many Feet in the Bed? 22
    Suggestions for Classroom Use 22
        Journaling 22
    The Hershey's Kisses Subtraction Book 23
    Suggestions for Classroom Use 23
        Journaling 23
    Subtraction Action 23
    Suggestions for Classroom Use 24
        Journaling 24

Multiplication and Division ... 24
  One Hundred Hungry Ants ... 24
    Suggestions for Classroom Use ... 26
      Journaling ... 26
  Amanda Bean's Amazing Dream ... 27
    Suggestions for Classroom Use ... 27
      Journaling ... 29
  A Remainder of One ... 29
    Suggestions for Classroom Use ... 29
      Journaling ... 30
  2 × 2 = Boo ... 30
    Suggestions for Classroom Use ... 30
      Journaling ... 31
  Spaghetti and Meatballs for All! ... 31
    Suggestions for Classroom Use ... 32
      Journaling ... 32

Fractions ... 32
  The Wishing Club ... 32
    Suggestions for Classroom Use ... 32
      Journaling ... 33
  Full House: An Invitation to Fractions ... 33
    Suggestions for Classroom Use ... 34
      Journaling ... 34
  Piece = Part = Portion ... 34
    Suggestions for Classroom Use ... 34
      Journaling ... 35
  The Doorbell Rang ... 35
    Suggestions for Classroom Use ... 35
      Journaling ... 36
  Centipede's 100 Shoes ... 36
    Suggestions for Classroom Use ... 36
      Journaling ... 36

Works Cited ... 36
Children's Books Cited ... 37
Additional Titles ... 38

CHAPTER 4: Algebra ... 51

Algebra Expectations ... 51
Using Mathematics Literature ... 51
  The King's Chessboard ... 51
    Suggestions for Classroom Use ... 53
      Journaling ... 53
  The Number Devil: A Mathematical Adventure ... 53
    Suggestions for Classroom Use ... 54
      Journaling ... 54
  The Adventures of Penrose the Mathematical Cat ... 54

| Suggestions for Classroom Use 55
| Journaling 55
| *Math Curse* 56
| Suggestions for Classroom Use 56
| Journaling 57
| *Fractals, Googles and Other Mathematical Tales* 57
| Suggestions for Classroom Use 57
| Journaling 57
Works Cited 57
Children's Books Cited 58
Additional Titles 58

CHAPTER 5: Geometry 61

Geometry Expectations 62
Using Mathematics Literature 62
    Sir Cumference and the First Round Table 62
    Suggestions for Classroom Use 63
        Journaling 63
    Grandfather Tang's Story 63
    Suggestions for Classroom Use 63
        Journaling 66
    The Greedy Triangle 66
    Suggestions for Classroom Use 66
        Journaling 66
    Draw Me a Star 66
    Suggestions for Classroom Use 67
        Journaling 67
    Mummy Math: An Adventure in Geometry 68
    Suggestions for Classroom Use 68
        Journaling 68
Works Cited 69
Children's Books Cited 70
Additional Titles 70

CHAPTER 6: Measurement 75

Measurement Expectations 75
Using Mathematics Literature 76
    Twelve Snails to One Lizard: A Tale of Mischief and Measurement 76
    Suggestions for Classroom Use 76
        Journaling 77
    How Tall, How Short, How Faraway 77
    Suggestions for Classroom Use 77
        Journaling 78
    Clocks and More Clocks 78
    Suggestions for Classroom Use 78
        Journaling 79

  Millions to Measure 79
   Suggestions for Classroom Use 79
    Journaling. 80
  Alexander, Who Used to Be Rich Last Sunday 80
   Suggestions for Classroom Use 80
    Journaling. 80
 Works Cited 80
 Children's Books Cited 81
 Additional Titles. 81

CHAPTER 7: Data Analysis and Probability. 87
 Data Analysis and Probability Expectations 87
 Using Mathematics Literature 88
  Cloudy with a Chance of Meatballs 88
   Suggestions for Classroom Use 88
    Journaling. 89
  Tricking the Tallyman 89
   Suggestions for Classroom Use 89
    Journaling. 90
  If the World Were a Village 90
   Suggestions for Classroom Use 91
    Journaling. 91
  Lemonade for Sale 92
   Suggestions for Classroom Use 92
    Journaling. 93
  Do You Wanna Bet? 93
   Suggestions for Classroom Use 93
    Journaling. 94
 Works Cited 94
 Children's Books Cited 94
 Additional Titles. 94

CHAPTER 8: Any Literary Selection Can Be a Mathematics Selection 97
 Using Literature 97
  A Perfect Snowman 97
   Suggestions for Classroom Use 98
    Journaling. 98
  Beetle McGrady Eats Bugs 98
   Suggestions for Classroom Use 98
    Journaling. 100
  Olivia . . . and the Missing Toy 100
   Suggestions for Classroom Use 100
    Journaling. 101
  Swamp Angel 101
   Suggestions for Classroom Use 101
    Journaling. 101
  Chicken Soup 102

Suggestions for Classroom Use	102
Journaling	102
Children's Books Cited	102
Additional Titles	102

Appendix: Worksheets 109

Title Index 127

Author Index 131

Figures

Figure 1.1: Sources That Include Evaluative Instruments for Assessing Mathematics Literary Selections 2
Figure 1.2: Math Poetry 4
Figure 1.3: Informational Books 5
Figure 2.1: Using Literature 12
Figure 3.1: Hundred's Chart 18
Figure 3.2: More Counting Books 19
Figure 3.3: Structures of Problems 20
Figure 3.4: Types of Questions 25
Figure 3.5: Multiplication Table 27
Figure 4.1: Girls and Mathematics 52
Figure 4.2: Math Games and Activities 52
Figure 4.3: Math Riddles 56
Figure 4.4: Math Series 1 57
Figure 5.1: Polygon Names 67
Figure 5.2: Math Literature Authors 69
Figure 5.3: Math Series 2 69
Figure 6.1: Math Series (Measurement) 76
Figure 6.2: Web Sites for Working with Measurement 79
Figure 7.1: Tally Sheet 89
Figure 7.2: Frequency Table 90
Figure 7.3: Math Series 3 91
Figure 8.1: Succotash Recipe 99
Figure 8.2: Menu for Bug Café 99
Figure 8.3: Charting the Family's Progress 105

About the Authors

SUEANNE E. MCKINNEY, Ph.D. is an assistant professor of STEM Education and Professional Studies at Old Dominion University in Norfolk, Virginia. Her research interests include teaching mathematics in elementary high-poverty schools and developing mathematics teachers for high-poverty schools. She is currently the editor of *Teaching Children Mathematics*, *From the Classroom Department* and has received numerous teaching awards, such as the Virginia Council of Teachers of Mathematics, 2009 William C. Lowry University Teacher of the Year Award. She currently serves as a board member for the Virginia Council of Teachers of Mathematics and the Tidewater Council of Teachers of Mathematics. Dr. McKinney has published numerous articles focusing on teaching elementary mathematics in high-poverty schools.

KAAVONIA HINTON, Ph.D. is an assistant professor in the Darden College of Education at Old Dominion University in Norfolk, Virginia. She is the author of *Angela Johnson: Poetic Prose* and *Sharon M. Draper: Embracing Literacy* and co-author (with Gail K. Dickinson) of *Integrating Multicultural Literature in Libraries and Classrooms in Secondary Schools* and (with Katherine T. Bucher) of *Young Adult Literature: Exploration, Evaluation, and Appreciation*. Her reviews of young adult and children's literature are published regularly in *VOYA* and *ForeWord* Magazine.

Introduction

In 2000, the National Council of Teachers of Mathematics (NCTM), an international professional organization committed to excellence in the teaching and learning of mathematics, proposed an ambitious vision of a rigorous, high-quality mathematics learning environment with a clear and comprehensive goal to stimulate conversations and efforts for the improvement of mathematics teaching and mathematical competence for students in grades prekindergarten through 12 (NCTM 3–8). Recognizing that the majority of students nationwide were not learning mathematics with depth and understanding and that teachers were not cultivating a mathematics-rich environment in which learning with conceptual understanding is the norm, the NCTM developed the *Principles and Standards for School Mathematics* (PSSM) to serve as a foundation for the improvement of mathematics curricula, teaching, and learning. To date, a vast majority of classrooms continue to fall short in the implementation and direction of the standards, in part because most of these classrooms continue to use traditional methods for teaching mathematics (Hiebert; NCTM; Van De Walle).

Mathematics Literature in the Classroom and Library encourages teachers and librarians to use a nontraditional approach—children's literature—to address the PSSM in grades K–8. This alternative approach to teaching math will help students think deeply about concepts and engage in mathematics literacy. This book was written to introduce librarians and teachers to a variety of books and strategies, but it is only an introduction, as thousands of new books are published each year.

Organization of the Book

Chapter 1 explores the benefits of using literature in mathematics classrooms.

Chapter 2 discusses collaboration between librarians and mathematics teachers.

Chapters 3–7 focus on one specific NCTM content standard and contain the following sections:

- Brief introduction that highlights the specific NCTM content standard featured;
- A *Suggested Title* section that offers a synopsis of several books;
- Several research-based instructional activities for integrating NCTM's process standards (i.e., problem solving, reasoning and proof, communication, connections, and representation);
- A journal prompt that suggests opportunities for research, critical thinking, and communication; and
- An annotated list of additional books that can be used to address the NCTM content standard featured in the chapter.

Chapter 8 shows how a teacher or librarian can turn any literature selection into an opportunity for mathematical investigations.

A complete outline of the NCTM standards is available in *Principles and Standards for School Mathematics* (NCTM). The activities promote interaction and motivation, yet they were written so that substitutions can be made if the school library does not have the books mentioned.

The additional titles are arranged alphabetically and include the author, title, illustrator, publisher, publication date, and a brief annotation. If the book is a part of a series, we have included the series title in parenthesis after the book title. All of the books are available at school and public libraries and bookstores.

An appendix is filled with reproducible worksheets. Two indexes are included: a title index, including all children's books recommended throughout the book, and an index of children's book authors.

How were the Books Selected?

Books were selected for their literary quality, mathematical accuracy, and relationship to the NCTM content standard featured in the chapters. Titles were chosen from journal articles, reviewer's lists, and the authors' research and teaching experiences. Once a book was considered, the authors searched Bowker's Books in Print and read book reviews of the book published in *School Library Journal, Library Media Connection,* or *Booklist* to determine if the book should be suggested to librarians and teachers. Recommended grade levels were derived from (1) book reviews and (2) the NCTM's expectations that a book could meet. Though we realize some of the books are appropriate for preschoolers, we indicate only grades K–8.

The books were in print (or had been reprinted) at the time of this writing. We have included both classic and new books. We realize that most of the books do not fit neatly in the chapters we have placed them in, as some books focus on more than one NCTM content standard. For example, while we put Kathryn Lasky's *The Librarian Who Measured the Earth* (1994) in the geometry chapter, it could have also gone in the measurement chapter.

The suggested books—picture books, illustrated books, chapter books, and novels—span several genres, including:

✦ Poetry;

✦ Informational texts;

✦ Fiction;

✦ Biography;

✦ Folktales;

✦ Fairytales; and

✦ Legends.

There are as many ways to use these books as there are suggested titles. Here are a few ways teachers and librarians have used them in math classrooms:

✦ Read-alouds;

✦ Shared reading;

✦ Whole-class study;

- Independent study;
- Silent reading; and
- Efferent reading.

What about Language Arts?

Using the books suggested in *Mathematics Literature in the Classroom and Library* makes it possible to achieve some important language arts–related goals:

- Cultivating lifelong readers;
- Impacting speaking and listening skills;
- Introducing different genres;
- Developing reading comprehension skills;
- Interpreting visual images; and
- Encouraging writing.

Appreciating Equity and Diversity

The National Council of Teachers of Mathematics has brought attention to the need for teachers to appreciate and honor equity and diversity in the mathematics classroom: "All students, regardless of their personal characteristics, backgrounds, or physical challenges, must have opportunities to study—and support to learn mathematics" (NCTM 12). Appreciating equity and diversity in the mathematics classroom requires teachers and librarians to demonstrate high expectations and provide worthwhile learning experiences for all students (NCTM 12). Further, accommodations and modifications need to be made if necessary so that all students can learn mathematics with understanding (NCTM 13). Support for mathematics learning must also be offered (NCTM 14). *Mathematics Literature in the Classroom and Library* includes activities and resources that can be used to address diversity in the mathematics classroom, highlighting specific strategies and authentic projects to effectively teach all students. Such equitable practices include:

1. *Emphasizing learning profiles of students.* Mathematics learners have different learning preferences, which, if addressed through instruction, can maximize their conceptual understanding of the content presented. Many of the activities included in this book recognize the value of addressing the different learning profiles of students. For example, activities for using *How the Second Grade Got $8,205.50 to Visit the Statue of Liberty* (1992), by Nathan Zimelman, incorporates the use of manipulatives for teaching coin recognition and value. Numerous other selections also include activities that use manipulatives that will benefit the visual and kinesthetic learner. For auditory learners, *Millions to Measure* (2003), by David M. Schwartz, includes an activity that uses hip-hop, rap, and pop music to teach students the metric system.

2. *Calling attention to contributions of people from different cultural backgrounds.* Different cultures have made contributions to the development of mathematical ideas (Akerman). For example, the ancient Egyptian calendar was first developed to inform the Egyptians when the Nile River would flood and serves as the basis for the Gregorian calendar

(O'Connor and Robertson 4). Also, Arabic mathematicians made significant contributions to algebra (O'Connor and Robertson 1–5). *Mathematics Literature in the Classroom and Library* exposes students to mathematical ideas contributed by different cultures, such as the measurement system of ancient Egypt and Rome and the Sieve of Eratosthenes algorithm, created by a Greek mathematician. Selections that highlight different countries and cultures are also included, such as *The King's Chessboard,* by David Birch, which takes place in India, and *If the World Were a Village,* by David J. Smith, which lay emphasis on the world's people.

3. *Highlighting readiness levels of students.* Teachers and librarians must respond to students' readiness level. Students bring with them different levels of sophistication in their understanding of different mathematical concepts and ideas. To support individual students' readiness levels, mathematical concepts need to be introduced at varying degrees of difficulty. *Mathematics Literature in the Classroom and Library* contains a variety of activities that range from multifaceted to less complex. For example, the Geometry chapter contains activities that engage students in using tangrams and in creating their own set.

4. *Providing a multitude of resources for teachers and librarians.* To provide all students with a high-quality mathematics instructional program, a variety of resources is needed. *Mathematics Literature in the Classroom and Library* includes a vast array of resources that can be used in the mathematics classroom. Such resources include teaching materials, Web sites that focus on specific concepts, and concrete and virtual manipulatives.

5. *Valuing ideas of students.* Creating a classroom climate that appreciates the ideas of students is necessary to maximize opportunities for learning mathematics. Journal questions included in *Mathematics Literature in the Classroom and Library* allow students to explore their creativity and research skills, while respecting the uniqueness of each child. For example, planning a spaghetti dinner for family members, or identifying mathematical ideas when building a snowman requires individual reflective thought, allowing students to connect prior mathematical learnings.

Addressing equity and diversity in the mathematics classroom is essential to meeting the mathematical needs of all learners. This includes providing a variety of mathematical opportunities that appreciates the uniqueness of each student and what they bring to the classroom learning environment. *Mathematics Literature in the Classroom and Library* helps educators accomplish this important goal.

Librarians and teachers who incorporate literature selections within their mathematics teaching invite students to experience and explore the real world of mathematics. *Mathematics Literature in the Classroom and Library* makes including literature easier, as it introduces dozens of children's books and activities for grades K–8 that are appropriate for teaching various mathematics content strands.

Works Cited

Akerman, Aimee. *Contributions of Different Cultures to the Growth and Development of Mathematical Ideas: An Internet Guide for Teachers.* 7 November 2009. <www.glis.utexas.edu/~vlibrary/edres/pathfinders/akerman/>.

Hiebert, James. "What Research Says about the NCTM Standards." In Jeremy Kilpatrick, W. Gary Martin, and Deborah. Schifter, eds. *A Research Companion to Principles and Standards for School Mathematics* (5–23). Reston, VA: National Council of Teachers of Mathematics, 2003.

National Council of Teachers of Mathematics. *Principles and Standards for School Mathematics.* Reston, VA: National Council of Teachers of Mathematics, 2000.

O'Connor, John, and Robertson, Edmund. *An Overview of Egyptian Mathematics.* 7 November 2009. <www.gap-system.org/~history/HistTopics/Egyptian_mathematics.html>.

O'Connor, John, and Robertson, Edmund. *History Topic: Arabic Mathematics: Forgotten Brilliance?* 2 November 2009. <www.gap-system.org/~history/PrintHT/Arabic_mathematics.html>.

Van De Walle, John, Karen Karp, and Jennifer Bay-Williams. *Elementary and Middle School Mathematics.* Boston: Allyn and Bacon, 2010.

Children's Books Cited

Birch, David. *The King's Chessboard.* Illus. Devis Grebu. New York: Puffin Books, 1988.

Lasky, Kathryn. *The Librarian Who Measured the Earth.* Illus. Kevin Hawkes. Boston: Little, Brown, 1994.

Schwartz, David. *Millions to Measure.* Illus. Steven Kellogg. New York: HarperCollins, 2003.

Smith, David J. *If the World Were a Village.* Illus. Shelagh Armstrong. Toronto: Canada: Kids Can Press, 2002.

Zimelman, Nathan. *How the Second Grade Got $8,205.50 to Visit the Statue of Liberty.* Illus. Bill Slavin. Morton Grove: IL: Albert Whitman and Company, 1992.

Chapter 1

Using Literature in the Mathematics Classroom and Library

Take a moment to reflect on your mathematical experiences in elementary and middle school. Was your classroom dominated by typical mathematics instruction that emphasized memorization and speed? Do you still get bouts of anxiety just thinking about those timed multiplication tests? Did your teacher follow a somewhat ritualistic schedule when introducing new mathematical skills and concepts—a routine that continues to be readily seen in many mathematics classrooms today? The routine probably looked something like this:

> First, answers were given for the previous day's assignment. A brief explanation, sometimes none at all, was given of the new material, and problems were assigned for the next day. The remainder of the class was devoted to students working independently on the homework while the teacher moved around the room answering questions. (Welch 6)

Whether this traditional approach to the teaching and learning of mathematics captures your experience as an elementary or middle school student, it is apparent that far too many students continue to be intimidated by mathematics and are not developing a conceptual understanding of the different mathematical ideas when this teaching methodology dominates the mathematics classroom (Hiebert 10–12). In fact, the National Research Council boldly states, "Much of the failure in school mathematics is due to a tradition of teaching that is inappropriate to the way most students learn" (6). With this in mind, what approaches should be used when teaching mathematics? What strategies work best in promoting the learning of mathematics with understanding? How can the teaching of mathematics move beyond the traditional approach? How can educators break the perception that mathematics is threatening and beyond reach for many students? Integrating children's literature with mathematics is one approach that can "restore the reputation" of mathematics as a content area that can be fun, exciting, and achievable for all.

Linking Mathematics and Literature

Teachers and librarians have become quite intrigued with the idea of using literature as a springboard for mathematics learning, and, as a result, integrating the two has become increasingly widespread (NCTM, *Exploring Mathematics* xi). However, linking children's literature to the teaching of mathematics is a bit more sophisticated than just reading a literary selection to students during mathematics instructional time (Schiro 1–3). More specifically, literature selections can be used as a catalyst to launch student interactions, discussions, and investigations that emphasize mathematical processes such as problem solving and reasoning skills. Linking children's literature to the teaching of mathematics can also connect the applications of mathematical ideas to authentic, everyday experiences.

Evaluating Mathematical Literature Selections

As stated earlier, integrating children's literature selections with mathematics has received much attention, and there is an abundance of books that can be used in the mathematics classroom. However, this popularity has also resulted in many selections that are not of high mathematical and literary integrity (Hellwig, Monroe, and Jacobs 139; Hunsader 620; NCTM, *Exploring Mathematics* xi). Teachers and librarians must carefully examine different selections to determine if a book is appropriate for teaching a specific mathematical concept (Halsey 159; Hunsader 620). To assist teachers and librarians, several educators have developed evaluative criteria that offer significant elements of a rich mathematics literary selection. For example, Hellwig, Monroe, and Jacobs suggest that educators should determine whether each book "represents mathematics and other information accurately; depicts relationships correctly," and "provides a context for learners to make meaningful connections between mathematics and their own experiences" (139). Figure 1.1 provides a list of sources that includes evaluative criteria and instruments. However, it is important to keep in mind how the literature selection will be used when teaching mathematics. For example, some books may be perfect to introduce a skill in mathematics but lack the necessary foundation for conceptual understanding of the skill.

Advantages of Linking Mathematics and Literature

The research and literature clearly documents the opportunities and advantages of infusing literature with mathematics (Burns; Burns and Sheffield; Capraro and Capraro; Ezell; Monroe and Livingston; NCTM, *Exploring Mathematics*; Wallace and Shivertaker 9–13; Ward, "Using Children's Literature"; Ward, "Literature-based Activities"; Whitin and Whitin; Whitin and Wilde; Wilburne and Napoli 6). Let's explore some of those advantages.

Hellwig, Stacey, Eula Monroe, and Jim Jacobs. "Making Informed Choices: Selecting Children's Trade Books for Mathematics Instruction." *Teaching Children Mathematics* 7.3 (2000): 138–143.

Schiro, Michael. *Integrating Children's Literature and Mathematics in the Classroom: Children as Meaning Makers, Problem Solvers, and Literary Critics*. New York: Teachers College Press, 1997.

Whitin, Phyllis, and David Whitin. *New Visions for Linking Literature and Mathematics*. Reston, VA: National Council of Teachers of Mathematics, 2004.

Figure 1.1 Sources That Include Evaluative Instruments for Assessing Mathematics Literary Selections

1. *Connects mathematics to the real world.* More often than not, mathematical ideas are presented as a body of isolated and abstract skills and procedures, with little or no relevance to students' informal knowledge or to authentic situations. Children's literature can present different mathematical ideas through realistic situations. Take, for example, *Minnie's Diner,* by Dayle Ann Dodds, which illustrates the concept of multiplication through the McFay family's lunch orders, or Lucy Coats's *Neil's Numberless World,* an excellent book that shows the necessity of numbers in everyday life and what might happen if numbers simply did not exist.

2. *Stimulates mathematical discourse among students.* When students are offered opportunities to participate in meaningful conversations, they learn to alter, modify, and expand on their existing understanding of mathematical concepts. "Math talk" also promotes a deeper understanding of the different mathematical ideas among students, engages them in metacognitive behavior, helps them develop appropriate terminology, and allows them to take ownership of their mathematics learning (Van De Walle 47). *Twelve Snails to One Lizard: A Tale of Mischief and Measurement,* by Susan Hightower, is one of many books for children that can be used to stimulate math talk. The book presents the reader with different animals (e.g., snails, iguanas, boa constrictors) that can be used as nonstandard units of measure. To stimulate mathematics discourse among students, you might consider the following types of questions based on the book:

   ✦ Do you think a snail would be an acceptable nonstandard unit to represent an inch? Why do you think as you do?

   ✦ How can we prove that 36 snails would represent 36 inches?

   ✦ How can we figure out how many snails would represent two yards? three yards?

3. *Provides an avenue for mathematical problem solving investigations.* The National Council of Teachers of Mathematics encourages the teaching of mathematics through problem solving. "Students should have frequent opportunities to formulate, grapple with, and solve complex problems that require a significant amount of effort and should be encouraged to reflect on their thinking" (NCTM, *Principles* 52). Problem solving is an essential component of developing a deep understanding of the different concepts and can be infused within many literary selections. *Math Curse,* by Jon Scieszka, presents a multitude of problem-solving situations such as measuring the Mississippi River with M&Ms and comparing the average modern baseball player to Babe Ruth.

   Other literature selections may not present specific problems that can lead to investigations. However, both the teacher and librarian can present problem-solving investigations based on any selection. For example, Aileen Friedman's *The King's Commissioners* introduces different counting methods. Students can be challenged to develop other counting methods to provide the King with an accurate number of his many royal commissioners.

4. *Provides illustrations that represent different mathematical concepts.* Many of the available literature selections provide models and pictorial formats to clearly represent the mathematical ideas presented, allowing students to connect abstract procedures and relationships with visual representations. Charlotte Huck's *A Creepy Countdown* introduces the numbers 1–10 to readers. Students will see that the illustrations depict a Halloween theme (e.g., skeletons, pumpkins, witches, and so on) to represent the identified numbers. Likewise, *The Hershey's Milk Chocolate Fraction Book,* by Jerry Pallotta, models the concept under study through illustrations depicting chocolate.

Baker, Keith. *Potato Joe*. Orlando, FL: Harcourt, 2008. (Grades K–1)

Bloom, Valerie. *Fruits: A Caribbean Counting Poem*. Illus. David Axtell. New York: Henry Holt, 1997. (Grades K–2)

Franco, Betsy. *Counting Our Way to the 100th Day!: 100 Poems*. Illus. Steven Salerno. New York: Margaret K. McElderry, 2004. (Grades K–2)

———. *Mathematickles!* Illus. Steven Salerno. New York: Margaret K. McElderry, 2003. (Grades 2–5)

Hopkins, Lee Bennett. *Marvelous Math: A Book of Poems*. Illus. Karen Barbour. New York: Simon and Schuster, 1997. (Grades 3–5)

Mannis, Celeste Davidson. *One Leaf Rides the Wind: Counting in a Japanese Garden*. Illus. Susan Kathleen Hartung. New York: Viking, 2002. (Grades K–2)

Michelson, Richard. *Ten Times Better: Poems and Text*. Illus. Leonard Baskin. New York: Marshall Cavendish, 2000. (Grades 3–6)

Rose, Deborah Lee. *The Twelve Days of Kindergarten: A Counting Book*. Illus. Carey Armstrong-Ellis. New York: Abrams, 2003. (Grades K–1)

Yolen, Jane. *Count Me a Rhyme: Animal Poems by the Numbers*. Illus. Jason Stemple. Honesdale, PA: Wordsong, 2006. (Grades 1–5)

———. *Shape Me a Rhyme: Nature's Forms in Poetry*. Illus. Jason Stemple. Honesdale, PA: Wordsong, 2007. (Grades 3–6)

Figure 1.2 Math Poetry

5. *Allows for the development of language and mathematical skills simultaneously.* Children's literature can promote mathematical skills and language skills when integrated. For example, different styles of poetry can be introduced using *Mathematicles!*, by Betsy Franco, and *Marvelous Math: A Book of Poems,* by Lee Bennett Hopkins. See Figure 1.2 for a list of books that contain math poetry. Responding to literature also enhances the practice of constructing meaning both with mathematics and with literacy. Writing, journaling, reflective tasks, and literature discussion groups are but a few strategies that can be used to connect mathematics with literacy learning (Cooper and Kiger 306–332).

6. *Introduces mathematical vocabulary.* There are a variety of literature books that introduce mathematical vocabulary through the context of a story, providing students with a reference that allows them to actually develop a conceptual base of the mathematical terminology. This is seen clearly in books like *Sir Cumference and the First Round Table,* by Cindy Neuschwander, which presents a link between mathematical terminology and characters in the story.

7. *Promotes positive dispositions about doing mathematics.* Because of the many benefits of using literature during mathematics instruction, students may begin to release any anxiety or attitudes that obstruct their learning. When students enjoy doing mathematics and gain confidence in their mathematical abilities, they become independent thinkers (Van De Walle 34). This allows for the development of latent talents, such as persistence, perseverance, and risk taking when doing mathematics.

Certainly, there are many advantages and endless possibilities when connecting mathematics with literature. Literary selections are not only rich sources for promoting mathematical understanding but also a means to create a new vision of how mathematics can be taught. See Figure 1.3 for a list of informational books.

Adams, Colleen. *Tangram Puzzles: Describing and Comparing Attributes of Plane Geometric Shapes* (PowerMath). New York: PowerKids, 2004. (Grades 3–6)

Long, Lynette. *Painless Geometry* (Painless). Illus. Tom Kerr. Hauppauge, NY: Barron's, 2001. (Grade 8)

Wingard-Nelson, Rebecca. *Algebra I and Algebra II* (Math Success). Berkeley Heights, NJ: Enslow, 2004. (Grades 7–8)

———. *Amusement Park Word Problems Starring Pre-Algebra: Math Word Problems Solved* (Math Word Problems Solved). Berkeley Heights, NJ: Enslow, 2009. (Grades 4–7)

———. *Data, Graphing, and Statistics* (Math Success). Berkeley Heights, NJ: Enslow, 2004. (Grades 4–8)

Wolk-Stanley, Jessica. *Learning Geometry Is Easy!: Dr. Math Gets You Ready for Geometry.* Hoboken, NJ: Wiley, 2003. (Grades 7–8)

———. *Learning Pre-algebra Is Easy!: Dr. Math Gets You Ready for Algebra.* Hoboken, NJ: Wiley, 2003. (Grades 7–8)

Figure 1.3 Informational Books

Linking Mathematics with Writing

The NCTM publication *Principles and Standards for School Mathematics* identifies *Communication* as one of the Process Standards for mathematics learning (60). Communication in the mathematics classroom involves the provision of opportunities for students to share their mathematical understanding and ideas orally or in writing (NCTM 60). Journaling is one strategy that allows students to convey their understanding of different mathematical concepts, explore and test these concepts in-depth and from different perspectives, and connect mathematics to authentic situations. Journaling can also assist students with organizing their ideas and thinking, making connections with mathematical symbols and words, and building a deeper conceptual understanding of different rules, algorithms, and procedures (NCTM 60–62).

We provide sample journaling and research questions for you to use with students as you introduce literature in the library or mathematics classroom. Many of the questions delve into student's understanding of the different mathematical ideas, while others provide an extension to intrigue student's interest in mathematics.

Works Cited

Burns, Marilyn. *Math and Literature (K–3).* Book One. Sausalito, CA: Math Solutions, 1992.

Burns, Marilyn, and Stephanie Sheffield. *Math and Literature.* Sausalito, CA: Math Solutions, 2004.

Capraro, Robert Michael, and Mary Capraro. "'Are You Really Going to Read Us a Story?' Learning Geometry through Children's Mathematics Literature." *Reading Psychology* 27.1 (2006): 21–36.

Cooper, J. David, and Nancy Kiger. *Literacy: Helping Students Construct Meaning.* Boston: Houghton Mifflin Company, 2009.

Ezell, Michelle. "Integrating Literature into Mathematics Instruction: Literature Review." Educational Resources Information Center. 3 Jan. 2009.

Halsey, Pamela. "Assessing Mathematics Tradebooks: Do They Measure Up?" *Reading Improvement* 42.3 (2005): 158–163.

Hellwig, Stacey, Eula Monroe, and Jim Jacobs. "Making Informed Choices: Selecting Children's Trade Books for Mathematics Instruction." *Teaching Children Mathematics* 7.3 (2000): 138–143.

Hiebert, James. "What Research Says about the NCTM Standards." In Jeremy Kilpatrick, W. Gary Martin, and Deborah. Schifter, eds., *A Research Companion to Principles and Standards for School Mathematics* (5–23). Reston, VA: National Council of Teachers of Mathematics, 2003.

Hunsader, Patricia. "Mathematics Trade Books: Establishing Their Value and Assessing Their Quality." *The Reading Teacher* 57.7 (2004): 618–629.

Monroe, Eula Ewing, and Nancy Livingston. "It Figures: Language and Mathematics Add up through Children's Literature." *The Dragon Lode* 2.20 (2002): 37–41.

National Council of Teachers of Mathematics. *Exploring Mathematics through Literature*. Reston, VA: National Council of Teachers of Mathematics, 2006.

———. *Principles and Standards for School Mathematics*. Reston, VA: National Council of Teachers of Mathematics, 2000.

National Research Council. *Everybody Counts: A Report to the Nation on the Future of Mathematics Education*. Washington, DC: National Research Council, 1989.

Schiro, Michael. *Integrating Children's Literature and Mathematics in the Classroom: Children as Meaning Makers, Problem Solvers, and Literary Critics*. New York: Teachers College Press, 1997.

Van De Walle, John, Karen Karp, and Jennifer Bay-Williams. *Elementary and Middle School Mathematics*. Boston: Allyn and Bacon, 2010.

Wallace, Faith H., and Jill Shivertaker. *Teaching Mathematics through Reading: Methods and Materials for Grades 6–8*. Worthington, OH: Linworth Publishing, 2009.

Ward, Robin. *Literature-based Activities for Integrating Mathematics with Other Content Areas*. Boston: Pearson, 2009.

———. "Using Children's Literature to Inspire K–8 Preservice Teachers' Future Mathematics Pedagogy." *The Reading Teacher* 59.2 (2005): 132–143.

Welch, Wayne. "Science Education in Urbanville: A Case Study." In R. Stakes and J. Easley, eds., *Case Studies in Science Education* (5–33). Urbana: University of Illinois Press, 1978.

Whitin, David, and Sandra Wilde. *Read Any Good Math Lately?* Portsmouth, NH: Heinemann, 1992.

Whitin, Phyllis, and David Whitin. *New Visions for Linking Literature and Mathematics*. Reston, VA: National Council of Teachers of Mathematics, 2004.

Wilburne, Jane, and Mary Napoli. "Connecting Mathematics and Literature: An Analysis of Pre-service Elementary School Teachers' Changing Beliefs and Knowledge." *IUMPST: The Journal, (Pedagogy)* 2 (2008): 1–10.

Children's Books Cited

Coats, Lucy. *Neil's Numberless World.* Illus. Neal Layton. New York: Dorling Kindersley Publishing, 2000.

Dodds, Dayle Ann. *Minnie's Diner: A Multiplying Menu.* Illus. John Manders. Cambridge, MA: Candlewick, 2004.

Franco, Betsy. *Mathematicles!* Illus. Steven Salerno. New York: Aladdin, 2003.

Friedman, Aileen. *The King's Commissioners* (Brainy Day Books). Illus. Susan Guevara. New York: Scholastic, 1994.

Hightower, Susan. *Twelve Snails to One Lizard: A Tale of Mischief and Measurement.* Illus. Matt Novak. New York: Simon and Schuster Books for Young Readers, 1997.

Hopkins, Lee Bennett. *Marvelous Math: A Book of Poems.* Illus. Karen Barbour. New York: Aladdin, 2001.

Huck, Charlotte. *A Creepy Countdown.* Illus. Jos. A. Smith. New York: Greenwillow, 1998.

Neuschwander, Cindy. *Sir Cumference and the First Round Table* (A Math Adventure Series). Illus. Wayne Geehan. Watertown, MA: Charlesbridge, 1997.

Pallotta, Jerry. *The Hershey's Milk Chocolate Fractions Book.* Illus. Rob Bolster. New York: Scholastic, 1999.

Scieszka, Jon. *Math Curse.* Illus. Lane Smith. New York: Viking, 1995.

CHAPTER 2

Collaborating with Mathematics Teachers

Librarians know that collaborating with content-area teachers helps enrich students' learning, and they have tried to spread the word. Many have heard and responded, but there are some who may need to be convinced. Scholars argue that mathematics teachers are least likely to collaborate with librarians, and they rarely use the school library's collection (Fitch 45; Gardner 26; Wallace 26; Wallace and Shivertaker 2). Those of us who know the value of collaboration shudder at the thought of all of those missed opportunities to better serve students. Mathematics teachers are not to blame. Perhaps, as Small suggests, content-area teachers were not trained to collaborate: "Pre-service teacher training has traditionally taught prospective educators to function within the confines of their four-walled classroom, collaborating strictly within confines of their disciplines or grade levels" (10). The amount of collaboration between mathematics teachers and librarians would increase if *both* professionals understood how working together could enhance mathematics instruction and lead to student achievement (Farmer 150).

There are different types and levels of collaboration. Collaboration may include "collaboratively brainstorming and developing plans for a teacher-taught unit; selecting materials (print, non-print and electronic) for use by teacher/students during an instructional unit; [or] coordinated teaching, with the classroom teacher focusing on content instruction and the teacher-librarian teaching information literacy skills as needed" (Schomberg 8). Here, we suggest that collaboration occurs when the mathematics teacher and librarian work together to plan instruction, teach content, and assess student learning (Hinton and Dickinson 20; Schomberg 8).

The American Association of School Librarians' *Standards for the 21st-Century Learner* maintains that librarians and teachers should work together to educate students. Researchers report that when this happens the effort promotes student achievement (Doll 26; Farmer 57).

One study described by Farmer indicated that students improved in math computation and other content areas when a school library media specialist was on the instructional team (38). Moreover, Lance, Welborn, and Hamilton-Pennell conclude, "Students whose library media specialists played . . . [an instructional] role—either by identifying materials to be used with teacher-planned instructional units or by collaborating with teachers in planning instructional units—tend to achieve higher average test scores" (93).

To Mathematics Teachers

Mathematics teachers may rarely enlist the help of a school librarian because they do not fully understand what librarians do or what a valuable resource librarians can be. As trained educational media specialists, librarians are knowledgeable about print and nonprint resources that span the curriculum, and they recommend these resources to students and teachers. Though librarians can suggest materials that can help enhance mathematics instruction, librarians are also teachers. As stated earlier, librarians can collaborate on every aspect of the instructional process, from brainstorming instructional strategies to assessing student learning. Librarians have access to a wealth of information: the course of study for mathematics, mathematics textbooks, and professional literature (including journals and magazines) of interest to a mathematics teacher (Gardner 27; Minkel 29). Librarians want to put this knowledge to use to help serve more students and teachers.

No one questions an English teacher who schedules a class visit to the library, but what about mathematics teachers? The library is a viable place for mathematics teachers to have class, too (Gardner 26). In fact, collaboration between librarians and mathematics teachers has led to rich educational experiences (see, for example, Gardner 26–28; Minkel 28). Fleming says, "Just as information-literacy skills lead to higher reading scores, practicing mathematics skills in the library strengthens students' abilities to apply and understand mathematics, which likely leads to higher math scores" (43). One of the easiest things you can do to begin laying ground for potential collaboration is take advantage of the school library. Here are a few things to consider:

✦ Visit the librarian when you are about to plan a new unit;

✦ Broaden your definition of a mathematics text and curriculum, and consider using children's literature, informational trade books, and environmental print;

✦ Look through your lesson plans and choose one that can be improved with collaboration;

✦ Assign library-based research projects;

✦ Incorporate databases, Web sites, and computer applications in your lessons;

✦ Encourage students to use the library productively;

✦ Drop into the library periodically. The librarian just might grab you and tell you about (or show you) a new resource; and

✦ Give your opinion. Librarians appreciate feedback about the value (or dearth) of sources (Fleming 43–44; Gardner 27–28; Minkel 29; Wallace 26).

To Librarians

Before reaching out to mathematics teachers, you will want to review the national and statewide standards related to mathematics. The NCTM's *Principles and Standards for School*

Mathematics articulates the new vision of a high-quality mathematics classroom and identifies the principles, process, and content standards for teaching mathematics.

Next, survey your collection to reacquaint yourself with what your school library has to offer a mathematics teacher and her students. For example, do databases include a focus on mathematics skills? Also, look at fiction and nonfiction holdings to see if the titles are suitable for the study of mathematics (Fleming 43–44). Mathematical relationships can be drawn from a variety of fiction and nonfiction titles, but check to see if the collection has books that contain tables, graphs, and charts (Fleming 43).

The mathematics teacher is busy inside her own classroom. She is organizing manipulatives, pulling out calculators and textbooks, and turning on the Smartboard, so she might not think about the library at all. A librarian who wants to change this can start by doing several things:

- Ask if you can attend mathematics department meetings so that you can ascertain their needs, get advice on the purchase of specific sources, introduce online reference tools, and demonstrate the use of Web sites relevant to the study of mathematics;
- Offer to display information about new print titles related to mathematics in classrooms;
- Offer to serve on committees within the mathematics department;
- Listen to students talk about what (and how) they are learning in mathematics classes, and use the information to reach out to the mathematics teacher; and
- Invite mathematics teachers to the library. (Minkel)

Once you have gotten teachers' attention, get to know them and help them understand how you can help. Initially, you might observe them while they teach so that you can look for ways that your resources and instructional skills will help enhance their lesson (Gardner 26). Sitting together at lunch or at other times when chatting is possible will give you an opportunity to learn more about the mathematics teacher's philosophy of teaching (Minkel 29). During your conversations with the mathematics teacher, give a brief overview of how you can help teachers develop technology skills, use databases and online resources, and discover materials and resources such as children's literature that can help them move beyond the mathematics textbook. After chatting several times, you will probably be better able to ascertain the types of materials you and the mathematics teacher might view as useful (Minkel 29).

When one thinks of the school librarian, booktalks, book displays, bulletin boards, and research come to mind. These tried and true strategies can be used for promoting literacy and mathematics. Librarians have revised these "old faithfuls" in various ways. For example, Fleming added mathematics to his introductory lesson on *The Hobbit* by J.R.R. Tolkien. He posed mathematics-related questions about Tolkien's life—how old was Tolkien when he published *The Hobbit?* how many years passed between the writing of *The Hobbit* and *The Fellowship of the Ring?*—while introducing the book (43). Though Fleming was addressing a language arts class, the same strategy can be used when doing an introductory lesson or a booktalk for a book in a mathematics class. Other librarians compile booklists and create book displays and bulletin boards filled with titles that work well with the mathematics curriculum. Still others assist teachers who require students to research mathematicians and investigate math-related concepts (Bernstein 17). Figure 2.1 lists some of the goals librarians and math teachers can accomplish using math literature.

Using literature in the classroom suggests that the librarian and the math teacher will work together to:

✦ Provide access to age and developmentally appropriate books;

✦ Introduce and reinforce math concepts;

✦ Connect math with other content areas;

✦ Encourage library-centered investigations;

✦ Foster written and verbal response to texts; and

✦ Promote reading. (Doll 4, 26; Farmer 38, 50, 157; Hellwig, Monroe, and Jacobs 139)

Figure 2.1 Using Literature

The teacher and librarian must work together to determine an appropriate way to evaluate student learning. Once the evaluative tool is selected, the math teacher will assess students' learning of mathematical concepts as related in the literature, while the school librarian will assess students' grasp of the information skills taught (Doll 4). While the activities in this book can be facilitated by the librarian alone, they can also be used to promote collaboration between the librarian and the mathematics teacher. The list of possibilities for working together is endless.

Works Cited

American Association of School Librarians. *Standards for the 21st-Century Learner*. http://www.ala.org/ala/mgrps/divs/aasl/guidelinesandstandards/learningstandards/standards.cfm. 31 July 2009.

Bernstein, Allison T. "Math Classes + the LMC = A Great Combination!" *Technology Connection* 4 (1998): 17. *ERIC* database. 7 Feb. 2009.

Doll, Carol. A. *Collaboration and the School Library Media Specialist*. Lanham, MD: Scarecrow, 2005.

Farmer, Lesley S. J. *Student Success and Library Media Programs: A Systems Approach to Research and Best Practice*. Westport, CT: Libraries Unlimited, 2003.

Fitch, Katherine. "Bulls and Bears." *School Library Journal* 45.5 (1999): 45. Education Full Text. 14 Jan. 2009.

Fleming, Dan. "Let Me Count the Ways." *School Library Journal* 50.8 (2004): 42–44. Education Full Text. 14 Jan. 2009.

Gardner, Judy. "Technology + Planning + Math = Integration." *Knowledge Quest* 32.5 (2004): 26–29. Education Full Text. 14 Jan. 2009.

Hellwig, Stacey, Eula Monroe, and Jim Jacobs. "Making Informed Choices: Selecting Children's Trade Books for Mathematics Instruction." *Teaching Children Mathematics* 7.3 (2000): 138–143.

Hinton, KaaVonia, and Gail K. Dickinson. *Integrating Multicultural Literature in Libraries and Classrooms in Secondary Schools*. Worthington, OH: Linworth, 2007.

Lance, Keith Curry, Lynda Welborn, and Christine Hamilton-Pennell. *Impact of School Library Media Centers on Academic Achievement*. Salt Lake City, UT: Hi Willow Research and Publishing, 1993.

Minkel, Walter, ed. "Hardly Rocket Science: Collaboration with Math and Science Teachers Doesn't Need to Be Complicated." *School Library Journal* 50.2 (2004): 28–29. Education Full Text. 14 Jan. 2009.

Schomberg, Janie. "TAG Team: Collaborate to Teach, Assess and Grow." *Teacher Librarian* 31.1 (2003): 8–11. Library Literature and Information Science Full Text. 14 Jan. 2009.

Small, Ruth V. "Collaboration: Where Does It Begin?" *Teacher Librarian* 29.5 (2002): 8–11. Library Literature and Information Science Full Text. 14 Jan. 2009.

Wallace, Faith H. "Reading Mathematics in the Middle Grades." *Library Media Connection* 27.1 (2008): 26–28. Library Literature and Information Science Full Text. 17 Jan. 2009.

Wallace, Faith H., and Jill Shivertaker. *Teaching Mathematics through Reading: Methods and Materials for Grades 6–8*. Worthington, OH: Linworth Publishing, 2009.

Chapter 3

Number and Operations

Number and Operations standards are crucial to teachers and librarians, as they encompass a wide variety of mathematical skills and understandings. Real-world experiences should be offered so that students can construct and interpret number meanings. Educators typically focus on teaching young students to count and to recognize a model representation of each number, but they also need to concentrate on developing students' number sense—intuitive sense about numbers—so that students will have a solid foundation for understanding the different relationships among numbers (NCTM 33).

As students progress toward developing meanings of different operations, such as addition, subtraction, multiplication, and division, they need teachers and librarians to help them move beyond the simple ideas behind the operations. For example, different types of addition and subtraction problems (i.e., join, separate, part-part-whole, and compare) need to be introduced to students in order to aid in their development of number sense (Van De Walle 146). Likewise, students need a conceptual understanding of the multiplication facts. Reciting facts based on rote learning has little meaning to students. Instructors must have a clear understanding of these ideas in order to share them with students.

Many young students struggle with fractions, and often this problem follows them to other grade levels (Van De Walle 286). Students tend to struggle with fractions repeatedly when fraction concepts are taught as a set of isolated rules and procedures without meaning. There is a rule for adding and subtracting fractions with like denominators and another for unlike denominators. There are also rules for working with improper fractions and with mixed numbers, multiplying and dividing fractions, reducing fractions, and finding equivalent fractions. No wonder children dislike fractions! However, providing experiences and learning opportunities that focus on relationships and differences among and between fractions and whole numbers will offer students a holistic view of fractions (Van De Walle 287).

Number and Operations Expectations

According to the Number and Operations standards, students need a strong understanding of numbers, number relationships, and number systems. This includes the ability to:

- Count;
- Understand place value;
- Represent whole numbers;
- Understand and represent fractions, decimals, percents, and ratios and proportions;
- Grasp integers;
- Square and determine square roots; and
- Analyze algorithms. (NCTM 78, 148, 214)

Students also need a sound conceptual and procedural understanding of the different operations and properties, including addition, subtraction, multiplication, and division. Computation fluency and estimation skills are expected of students, as well. A complete outline of the Number and Operations standards is available in *Principles and Standards for School Mathematics* (NCTM 78, 148, 214).

Counting

Children need to be given opportunities to gain an understanding of numbers and the different operations associated with them early and often. As they develop counting skills, they must attach meaning to the concept. This can be achieved through practice, support, and guidance (Van De Walle 127). As students develop counting skills and number sense, they should be provided activities that emphasize:

- Numeral writing and recognition,
- Counting on and counting back,
- Relationships among numbers, and
- Skip counting.

Using a variety of counting books assists students in developing these skills (Cathcart, Pothier, Vance, and Bezuk 81–84).

Using Mathematics Literature
A Creepy Countdown (1998) by Charlotte Huck

(Grades K–1) The scratchboard with watercolor illustrations creates a spooky mood just right for counting up to 10 scary creatures (e.g., ghosts, bats, witches). Once the creatures appear, they get a tremendous scare that frightens them, giving the reader the opportunity to count back as the scary things return to their original places.

Fish Eyes: A Book You Can Count On (1990) by Lois Ehlert

(Grades K–1) This counting book takes readers to the sea, where they can count up to 10 beautifully colored fish.

One Less Fish (1998) by Kim Michelle Toft and Allan Sheather

(Grades K–1) This book begins with 12 fish and counts down to 0, as subtraction is used to communicate what will happen to the ecosystem if it is destroyed. The authors also provide interesting facts and information about protecting the ocean's ecosystem.

The M&M's Count to One Hundred Book (2003) by Barbara Barbieri McGrath

(Grades K–3) This counting selection uses different color M&Ms to introduce counting from 1 to 100. Skip counting by 2s, 5s, and 10s is also introduced.

Dreaming: A Countdown to Sleep (2000) by Elaine Greenstein

(Grades K–1) *Dreaming* is a bedtime story that introduces numbers from 10 down to 1.

Suggestions for Classroom Use

Because all of the selections mentioned focus on counting, the following suggestions are appropriate for each book.

1. Relational ideas such as "more," "less," and "same" are usually developed before students enter school. However, students tend to struggle with the concept of "less" when compared to "more" (Van De Walle 126). When using any of the selections, ask questions that pertain to the illustrations, such as "Are there more striped fish or spotted fish?" Follow up with the question "Are there less spotted fish or striped fish?" Next, ask the students to construct their own illustrations based on the items found in the books. Tell them that the items in their illustrations must be arranged to represent "more," "less," and "same."

2. It is important for students to attach meaning to numbers and to match numbers with objects. This can be accomplished by allowing students to create their own counting books with numbers and the corresponding amount of objects.

3. Skip counting provides students with counting practice and early exposure to seeing patterns in numbers. Provide the students with a hundreds chart similar to the one in Figure 3.1.

4. Identify a starting point and direction. Students should practice skip counting by 2s, 5s, 10s, and other identified values.

1	2	3	4	5	6	7	8	9	10
11	12	13	14	15	16	17	18	19	20
21	22	23	24	25	26	27	28	29	30
31	32	33	34	34	36	37	38	39	40
41	42	43	44	45	46	47	48	49	50
51	52	53	54	55	56	57	58	59	60
61	62	63	64	65	66	67	68	69	70
71	72	73	74	75	76	77	78	79	80
81	82	83	84	85	86	87	88	89	90
91	92	93	94	95	96	97	98	99	100

Figure 3.1 Hundred's Chart

5. There are a variety of manipulatives that can be used to help students improve their counting skills. A few include:
   1. Counting Cookies: Ten cookies with counting chips represented on the top and the corresponding number written on the bottom are included in a plastic cookie jar. The cookies represent numbers 1–10.
   2. Fun Fish Counters: A set of 60 detailed fish counters come in 12 authentic shapes. Teachers and librarians can choose from a variety of counters, including people counters, teddy bear counters, frog counters, and mini-motor counters, to name a few. Browse the other available manipulatives at <http://www.etacuisennaire.com>.
6. Mathematics and music have an intriguing connection, and many researchers have concluded that music enhances mathematical abilities within students (Reid 1). There are many resources available for teachers and librarians that connect music with mathematics. A few that concentrate on the concept of counting include:
   1. *Mother Goose: Five Little Monkeys Counting Songs* (Soundprints)
   2. *Kids Sing and Learn: Numbers and Counting* (Calvin Records)

Journaling: Ask students to write about the following: How would our lives be different if there were no numbers? *Neil's Numberless World,* by Lucy Coats, tackles this question. Neil does not like numbers, but, the day they all disappear, his world changes dramatically: mail cannot be delivered, and his mother burns his birthday cake because she does not know what temperature to turn the oven to. Needless to say, Neil finally finds an appreciation for numbers. For more counting books, see Figure 3.2.

Addition and Subtraction

The processes of addition and subtraction involve four different types of relationships: join problems, separate problems, part-part-whole problems, and compare problems.

In a join problem, different quantities are being added or joined. The starting amount, change amount, and resulting amount represent the three quantities involved in this type of problem. In separate problems, a quantity is being removed. Part-part-whole problems

Brown, Margaret Wise. *Goodnight Moon 1, 2, 3: A Counting Book.* Illus. Clement Hurd. New York: HarperCollins, 2008. (Grade K)

Child, Lauren. *Charlie and Lola's Numbers* (Charlie and Lola). Cambridge, MA: Candlewick, 2007. (Grade K)

Duke, Kate. *One Guinea Pig Is Not Enough.* New York: Dutton, 1998. (Grades K–3)

Koller, Jackie French. *One Monkey Too Many.* Illus. Lynn M. Munsinger. San Diego: Harcourt, 1999. (Grades K–1)

Merriam, Eve. *Ten Rosy Roses.* Illus. Julia Gorton. New York: HarperCollins, 1999. (Grade K)

———. *12 Ways to Get to 11.* Illus. Bernie Karlin. New York: Simon & Schuster, 1993. (Grades K–1)

O'Keefe, Susan Heyboer. *One Hungry Monster: A Counting Book in Rhyme.* Illus. Lynn M. Munsinger. Boston: Little, Brown, and Co., 1989. (Grades K–3)

Ryan, Pam Muñoz, and Jerry Pallotta. *The Crayon Counting Book.* Illus. Frank Mazzola Jr. Watertown, MA: Charlesbridge, 1997. (Grade K)

Winter, Jeanette. *Josefina.* San Diego: Harcourt, 1996. (Grades K–2)

Wise, William. *Ten Sly Piranhas: A Counting Story in Reverse (A Tale of Wickedness—And Worse!).* Illus. Victoria Chess. New York: Penguin, 2004. (Grades K–2)

Figure 3.2 More Counting Books

involve two quantities that are combined into a whole, while compare problems compare two quantities (Cathcart et al., 127–128; Van De Walle 146–147). It is critical that all of these structures of problems are highlighted during instruction. See Figure 3.3.

How the Second Grade Got $8,205.50 to Visit the Statue of Liberty (1992) by Nathan Zimelman

(Grades 2–4) Susan Olson, treasurer and reporter of the second-grade class at Newton Barnaby, details each profit and loss accrued while she and fellow students try to raise money for a class trip to the Statue of Liberty. After the students sell lemonade, babysit, dogwalk, and help catch bank robbers, their distraught parents contribute the money needed to take the trip.

Suggestions for Classroom Use

1. The story includes the expense and profit amounts for each fundraising activity. The second graders' expenses for the paper drive include $2.00 to borrow a wagon, $10.00 to retrieve comic books, and $5.00 to pay for a ticket. Their profit is $13.00. Teachers and librarians can use the information included in this selection to pose the different types of addition and subtraction problem structures (join, separate, part-part-whole, and compare problems). For example, a teacher or librarian might ask: What is the total amount of their expenses? If their profit was $13.00 and their expenses were $17.00, how much did they make from the paper drive?

2. Students will have a blast planning their own trip! Bring in travel brochures from a local travel agency, or have the students search the Internet for a place that they would like to travel to. Help them identify the amount of money needed for the trip by actually

Join Problems	
Type	**Number Sentence**
Result Unknown Joe has 3 pieces of candy. Patty gave him 4 more pieces of candy. How many pieces of candy does Joe have now?	3 + 4 = ?
Change Unknown Joe had 5 pieces of candy. Patty gave him some more. Now Joe has 8 pieces of candy. How many pieces did Patty give him?	5 + ? = 8
Start Unknown Joe had some pieces of candy. Patty gave him 6 more. Now Joe has 9 pieces of candy. How many pieces of candy did Joe have to begin with?	? + 6 = 9
Separate Problems	
Result Unknown Joe had 6 pieces of candy. He gave 4 pieces to Patty. How many pieces of candy does Joe have now?	6 − 4 = ?
Change Unknown Joe had 7 pieces of candy. He gave some to Patty. Now Joe has 3 pieces left. How many pieces of candy did Joe give to Patty?	7 − ? = 3
Start Unknown Joe had some pieces of candy. He gave Patty 2 pieces. Now Joe has 5 pieces. How many pieces of candy did Joe have to begin with?	? − 2 = 5
Part-Part-Whole	
Whole Unknown Joe has some pieces of candy. 3 are sour balls and 2 are lollipops. How many pieces of candy does Joe have?	3 + 2 = ?
Part Unknown Joe has 8 pieces of candy. 3 are sour balls and the rest are lollipops. How many lollipops does Joe have?	3 + ? = 8
Compare Problems	
Difference Unknown Joe has 5 pieces of candy, and Patty has 2 pieces of candy. How many more pieces does Joe have than Patty?	2 + ? = 5
Larger Unknown Patty has 4 pieces of candy. Joe has 2 more pieces than Patty. How many pieces of candy does Joe have?	4 + 2 = ?
Smaller Unknown Joe has 9 cookies. He has 6 more than Patty. How many cookies does Patty have?	6 + ? = 9

Adapted from Cathcart, Pothier, Vance, and Bezuk 127–128.

Figure 3.3 Structures of Problems
From *Mathematics in the K–8 Classroom and Library* by Sueanne McKinney and KaaVonia Hinton. Santa Barbara, CA: Linworth. Copyright © 2010.

investigating the expenses. For example, they can search the airlines for a plane ticket and research the cost of hotels, restaurants, and other things they would have to pay for while on the trip. This activity will not only reinforce addition skills using money but also highlight estimation and budgeting skills.

3. Allow students to plan, organize, and conduct a classroom fundraiser. This activity will highlight both addition and subtraction, as students will need to track their profits and expenses.

4. This literature selection provides a wonderful opportunity to introduce money to students. Students come to school with a wide range of abilities to understand coin recognition and value. When teaching the concept of money, many teachers find it more effective to work with actual coins. However, money manipulatives are available, <www.etacuisenaire.com> and look quite realistic. Provide opportunities that focus on coin equivalencies and represent amounts with different coins. For example, 55¢ can be represented in various ways: two quarters and one nickel; five dimes and one nickel; and 55 pennies.

5. Students can take pleasure in a classroom shopping spree. This is especially fun at Christmas time. Bring in flyers, advertisements, and catalogs from the local mall or stores. Provide the students with a set amount of money, and allow them to develop a list of items they would like to purchase with the given amount of money.

Journaling: Encourage students to write about the following: Suppose you wanted to raise $100.00 (any value can be used here) to purchase a new video game. What are some ways that you can raise the money? If you are offering any services, what will you charge? How long do you think it will take you to raise that amount?

The Grapes of Math (2001) by Greg Tang

(Grades 2–6) *The Grapes of Math* introduces students to clever ways to help them add. Using math puzzles and riddles, the author highlights strategies for problem solving, such as using subtraction to add and looking for patterns. The charming puzzles are written in rhymes, and students will be amused at the clever and witty short poems. Tang's book is a must for any mathematics classroom or library.

Suggestions for Classroom Use

1. Ask the students to solve the different puzzles, and provide time for them to discuss their responses. To highlight the problem-solving process, have the students identify the strategy they used to solve the puzzle and explain why that was an appropriate strategy.

2. Students will have fun generating their own math puzzles. Using the puzzles developed by Tang as examples, encourage students to generate their own puzzles using one of the strategies presented in the book, complete with illustrations.

3. To introduce addition at the concrete level, counting manipulatives can be used. Have the students represent each of the puzzles with manipulatives and practice the new strategies being introduced.

4. Give students time to practice with the different thinking strategies for working with the basic facts of addition. These strategies include Adding One (adding one is the same as identifying the next counting number), Counting On (counting on from one addend; 6 + 2, can be looked at as 6, and 7, and 8), and Near Doubles (using doubles as a reference point; if students know 8 + 8 = 16, they can reason that 7 + 9 also equals 16).

5. Greg Tang has written other literary selections that emphasize problem solving through math puzzles: *Math Potatoes, Math for All Seasons, Mathterpieces, Math Fables, The Best of Times, Math Appeal,* and *Math Fables Too.*

Journaling: Encourage students to write about the following: What strategies do you use when adding numbers?

How Many Feet in the Bed? (1991) by Diane Johnston Hamm

(Grades K–2) When a father awakens, his little girl asks, "How many feet in the bed?" He replies, "Two." But the little girl jumps in the bed, and now there are four feet. The story continues with other family members jumping in the bed, adding two feet as they do. Then, one by one, each of the family members get out of the bed until there are no feet in the bed. This selection can be used as a counting and an addition and subtraction book.

Suggestions for Classroom Use

1. Ask students to write an addition and subtraction problem for each of the situations presented in the story. For example, when the father and the little girl are in the bed, the addition problem would be 2 + 2 = 4. When learning the basic addition facts, students should have practice writing addition problems both vertically and horizontally, so it is important to require both formats from the students.

    2 + 2 = 4   2 + 2/4

2. Ask the students to determine the number of other body parts in the bed. For example, they can determine the number of hands in the bed or the number of fingers in the bed. Students should also write the addition and subtraction equations for these problems.

3. *How Many Feet in the Bed?* also provides an opportunity to help students practice skip counting by twos. The teacher and librarian can use the number of fingers or toes in the bed to practice skip counting by 10s.

4. To introduce more complex addition and subtraction facts, continue the story, adding more people in the bed. Again, have the students write addition and subtraction problems for each of the situations.

5. *How Many Feet in the Bed?* can be paired with Audrey Wood's *The Napping House*. Ask students to compare the total number of feet in the different beds.

Journaling: Ask the students to generate a similar type of story using their own family members to determine the number of feet in the bed.

The Hershey's Kisses Subtraction Book (2002) by Jerry Pallotta

(Grades K–2) This selection introduces students to subtraction using Hershey's Kisses candy. A clown presents basic subtraction facts through vividly illustrated pictures, and the number 0 is introduced. The author highlights vocabulary, such as equal, difference, and equation.

Suggestions for Classroom Use

1. Students will definitely find this activity sweet. Using Hershey's Kisses, have them model and solve each of the subtraction problems presented in this selection. Also, ask the students to generate an addition problem to check their work, thus emphasizing the relationship between addition and subtraction.

2. Jerry Pallotta also wrote *Hershey's Kisses Addition Book*. *Hershey's Kisses Addition Book* and *The Hershey's Kisses Subtraction Book* can be used interchangeably to help students understand that addition and subtraction are inverse operations.

3. Provide experiences for students to develop an understanding of the addition and subtraction property of 0 by giving them addition and subtraction problems with 0 being added and subtracted. Lead students to generalize the addition and subtraction property of 0.

4. Fact families, or related facts, can assist students in learning basic addition and subtraction facts. Allow students to generate pictorial models of problems with their Hershey's Kisses. Then ask the students to write the fact families for each of the models.

The fact family for this pictorial model is **3 + 2 = 5, 2 + 3 = 5, 5 − 3 = 2 and 5 − 2 = 3.**

5. Ask students to generate other subtraction problems not mentioned in the book and model them with their Hershey's Kisses.

Journaling: Encourage students to investigate the many different Hershey's Kisses that are available (e.g., dark chocolate kisses and kisses filled with caramel), and identify their favorite Kiss. To connect mathematics with science, students can compare the weight or density of the different types of kisses.

Subtraction Action (2000) by Loreen Leedy

(Grades K–3) Students will enjoy reading this comic book–style selection that includes seven short chapters. In one chapter, "Less Is Less," Otto dresses up like Little Red Riding Hood and goes to deliver cookies to Grandma's house. On the way, Little Red Riding Hood encounters several situations that require the subtraction of some of the cookies. Basic subtraction facts, subtracting with regrouping, and subtracting decimals are introduced. The author also includes basic subtraction problems students can complete.

Suggestions for Classroom Use

1. In "What's the Difference," Miss Prime introduces different items that communicate less, or the idea of subtraction (e.g., a diet book, a coupon, a reduce-speed road sign). Ask students to brainstorm other items in the real world that communicate less and subtraction.

2. The author includes scrambled equations for readers to solve (e.g., –, 6, 3, 9, =). Provide students with other equations to unscramble, and ask them to generate their own so that their peers can solve them.

3. To emphasize the different types of subtraction problems (i.e., result unknown, change unknown, start unknown), provide the students with a variety of problems that have missing minuends (first value) and missing subtrahends (number you are subtracting). Ex. **? − 3 = 5, 8 − ? = 4, 7 − 2 = ?**

4. Students can use their imagination to create their own comic book stories that focus on subtraction. They can even work together in collaborative teams to create a comic book.

5. Loreen Leedy's *Mission Addition* and *Subtraction Action* can be used interchangeably to communicate that addition and subtraction are inverse operations. Students can participate in similar activities with addition as they did with subtraction, such as drawing comic book stories that depict addition.

Journaling: Encourage students to write about the following: What strategies do you use when subtracting numbers?

Multiplication and Division

Multiplication and division involves four types of questions: equal groups, combinations, area, and comparisons.

- Equal groups involve both multiplication and division and the number of equal sets, groups, or parts.

- Combination problems involve the number of possible pairings or combinations of two sets. Area and array problems deal with finding the area of a rectangular region.

- Comparison problems involve multiplicatively comparing two quantities (Cathcart et al., 134–135; Van De Walle 154–156). See Figure 3.4 for a list of types of questions.

One Hundred Hungry Ants (1993) by Elinor J. Pinczes

(Grades 3–6) One hundred hungry ants are on their way to a picnic to gather food. Before they go, they decide to travel in a single line, but they stop when they realize this line formation will delay their arrival. They then line up in 2 rows of 50, 4 rows of 25, 5 rows of 20, and, finally, 10 rows of 10. Ironically, when the ants reach the picnic, they discover the food is all gone.

Equal-Groups Problems	
Type	**Number Sentence**
Whole-Unknown (Multiplication) Rick has 2 bags of marbles. There are 5 marbles in each bag. How many marbles does Rick have altogether?	$2 \times 5 = 10$
Size of Groups Unknown (Division) Rick has 18 marbles, and he wants to share them equally with his 6 friends. How many marbles will each friend receive?	$18 \div 6 = 3$
Number of Groups Unknown (Division) Rick has 20 marbles. He divided them equally into 5 bags. How many marbles are in each bag?	$20 \div 5 = 4$
Combination Problems	
Product Unknown (Multiplication) Dawn has 3 pairs of slacks and 4 blouses. How many different outfits can she make?	$3 \times 4 = 12$
Product Unknown (Division) How many pairs of slacks does Dawn need to make 8 different outfits using 4 blouses?	$8 \div 4 = 2$
Area Problems	
Area (Multiplication) What is the area of a 3 unit by 6 unit rectangle?	3 units × 6 units = 18 square units
Comparison Problems	
Product Unknown (Multiplication) Lisa has 3 cookies. Geno has 3 times as many cookies as Lisa. How many cookies does Geno have?	$3 \times 3 = 9$
Set Size Unknown (Division) Lisa has 21 cookies. She has 3 times as many cookies as Geno. How many cookies does Geno have?	$21 \div 3 = 7$
Multiplier Unknown (Division) Lisa has 14 cookies and Geno has only 7. How many times as many cookies does Lisa have compared to Geno?	$14 \div 7 = 2$

Adapted from Cathcart, Pothier, Vance, and Bezuk 134–135; Van De Walle 154–156.

Figure 3.4 Types of Questions
From *Mathematics in the K–8 Classroom and Library* by Sueanne McKinney and KaaVonia Hinton. Santa Barbara, CA: Linworth. Copyright © 2010.

Suggestions for Classroom Use

1. This selection clearly shows the relationship between multiplication and division. Ask the students to figure out different line combinations if there were 20 ants, 30 ants, 40 ants, and so on. Next, ask students to write multiplication and division problems that justify their thinking.

   Ex.

   $8 \times 10 = 80$

   $8 \times 100 = 800$

   $8 \times 1{,}000 = 8{,}000$

   $80 \times 10 = 800$

   $80 \times 100 = 8{,}000$

   Students will be able to see the pattern that occurs when multiplying powers of 10. For example, when multiplying any number by 10, attach one 0 to it. When multiplying a number by 100, attach two 0s to it. To multiply any numbers that are multiples of 10, multiply the non-0 digits, then add on as many 0s as there are in the problem. Students can practice their mental math skills with this strategy!

2. Share with the students that one strategy for learning multiplication facts is drawing arrays of the problem. Show them how to draw an array for the problem 4×3. First draw four circles (any shape) across, and then draw three circles down (you can use the first circle you drew for 4 to count as the first circle you draw for 3). Have the students fill in the array to solve the problem. Students will see that $4 \times 3 = 12$.

   Ex.

   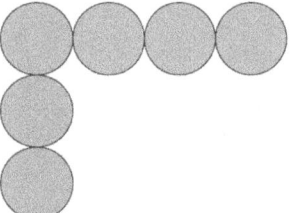 

3. Encourage students to create their own multiplication table. This table will allow students to look for patterns and will assist them in mastering the basic facts. You can use this table the way you would use a coordinate map. Identify the numbers being multiplied (multiplicand—the number being multiplied, and the multiplier—the number being multiplied by; the term factor can also be used) using the top row and the far left column. The product rests where the two intersect. The problem $4 \times 3 = 12$ is illustrated in Figure 3.5.

   Students will see different patterns when using their multiplication table. The multiplication facts for nine reveal an interesting pattern. Notice that when the digits of the products are added, they equal 9. For example, $9 + 0 = 9$, $1 + 8 = 9$, $2 + 7 = 9$, and so on. Students can always check their products against the nine facts by figuring out if they equal nine.

   Journaling: Ask students to look for and write about other patterns they discover in the multiplication chart.

X	1	2	3	4	5	6	7	8	9
1	1	2	3	4	5	6	7	8	9
2	2	4	6	8	10	12	14	16	18
3	3	6	9	12	15	18	21	24	27
4	4	8	12	16	20	24	28	32	36
5	5	10	15	20	25	30	35	40	45
6	6	12	18	24	30	36	42	48	54
7	7	14	21	28	35	42	49	56	63
8	8	16	24	32	40	48	56	64	72
9	9	18	27	36	45	54	63	72	81

Figure 3.5 Multiplication Table

Amanda Bean's Amazing Dream (1998) by Cindy Neuschwander

(Grades 3–5) Amanda Bean loves math, and she loves to count *everything*! Since she is good at counting, Amanda does not think it is important to learn multiplication facts. One night, Amanda dreams sheep are riding bikes, and she wants to count their legs and the number of wheels on their bikes, but they whiz by her too fast. She learns from her dream that multiplication is a faster way of counting. Now Amanda Bean multiplies everything.

Suggestions for Classroom Use

1. Using the illustrations and presented questions in the selection, ask the students to generate the multiplication problems. For example, for the question "How many wheels have rolled by her?," the multiplication problem would be $8 \times 2 = 16$, since there are eight sheep on a bike with two wheels. You can reinforce the connection of repeated addition to multiplication by having the students also include the repeated addition problem $(2 + 2 + 2 + 2 + 2 + 2 + 2 + 2 = 16)$

2. Take your students on a "Math Walk" around your school's playground or building. Have them look for multiplication problems in their surroundings, as Amanda Bean did.

3. Learning the Lattice Algorithm will assist students when multiplying numbers with two or more digits. For the problem 32×24, you would create a two-by-two (because you are working with two-digit numbers) lattice. Write one factor of the problem at the top of the lattice and the other along the right side. Multiply one digit at a time, putting the product in each lattice. Notice that each lattice has to be completed with two digits, so if a product is just a one-digit number, you would put a 0 in front of it. First multiply 3×2, which equals 6, so write a 0 and a 6 in the coordinating lattice. Next multiply 2×2, which equals 4, and write a 0 and 4 in the lattice. Now multiply 3×4, which equals 12, and write a 1 and 2 in the lattice. Finally, multiply 2×4, which equals 8, and write a 0 and an 8 in the lattice. The last step is to add the digits along each diagonal (starting on the right hand side). For example, there is nothing to add to 8, so just write 8. Now add $4 + 0 + 2$, which equals 6. Next add $0 + 6 + 1$, which equals 7. Your answer is 768.

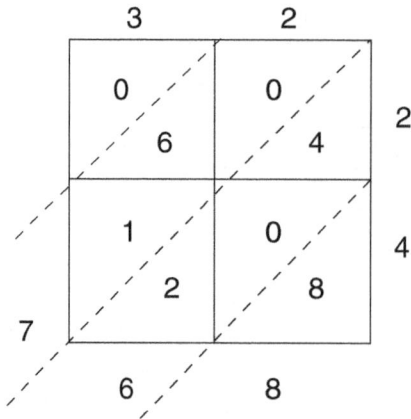

4. Introduce how to use base-10 blocks to solve multiplication problems. Base-10 blocks are manipulatives that assist students in developing a conceptual understanding of our standard number system. For the problem 10×11, display those factors along an axis using the blocks. If you multiply 10×10, which equals 100, you would fill the space with a 100 block. Then multiply 1×10, which equals 10, and put one 10 stick in the space. Add the base-10 manipulatives inside the axis. A template for the base-10 blocks is provided in the Appendix so that you can make your own set of manipulatives. Simply copy these on stock paper and cut them out. The different pictorials represent the ones, tens, and hundreds.

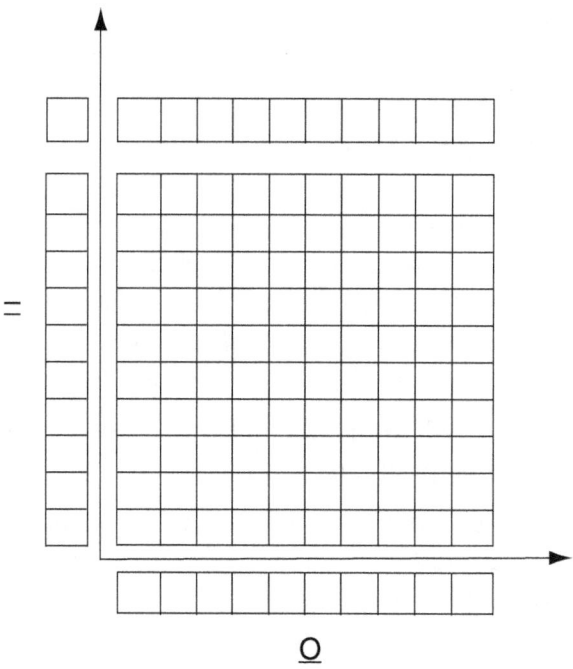

5. Students will be amazed with finger multiplication. Finger multiplication can be used to learn the nine facts. Display both your hands in front of you, with fingers spread apart. Each finger will represent a number from 1 to 10, 1 starting with your pinky finger on the left. If you want to multiply 2×9, bend your second finger. To determine the product, count the fingers to the left of the bent finger (1), and then count the fingers to the right of the bent finger (8). Your answer would be 18!

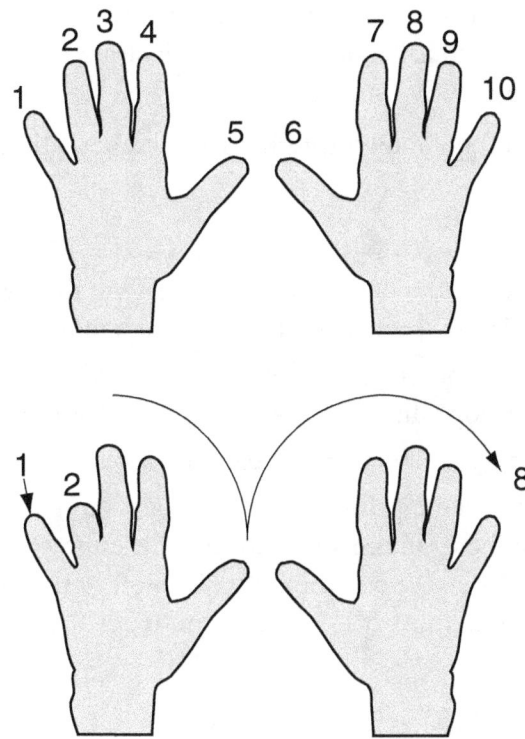

Journaling: Encourage students to write about the following: Do you think it was important for Amanda Bean to learn her multiplication facts instead of relying only on counting? Why? How and when do you use multiplication in everyday life?

A Remainder of One (1995) by Elinor J. Pinczes

(Grades 3–5) The 25th Squadron of bugs wants to please its queen, so it attempts to march orderly. Yet, each time the soldiers divide into even numbers, bug-soldier Joe is left to march alone behind the squad. Each night Joe tries to think of ways to divide the squad evenly, but, each day, he fails until he realizes he will not be a remainder of one if the soldiers march five in a row.

Suggestions for Classroom Use

1. The 25 ant soldiers line up in different configurations (e.g., two lines of 12, three lines of 8, four lines of 6), all resulting in Soldier Joe being a remainder. Offer students different total numbers of ant soldiers, and have them identify marching lines that will result in having a remainder.

2. The 24 Game is an excellent student-centered game that concentrates problem solving and reasoning skills. Students are presented with four numbers. They must use each number once in three equations. The three equations can be based on addition, subtraction, multiplication and division. The final answer of the third equation must equal 24.

    Division problems can be written in different ways $(6 \div 2 = 3;\ 2\overline{)6}^{\,3}\,;\ \text{and}\ 6/2 = 3)$.

    Allow students to practice solving division problems written in different formats.

3. Provide students with different counters or base-10 blocks. Present division problems that will have a remainder, and ask students to demonstrate those problems with the counters or base-10 manipulatives.

4. Casting out nines is a fun strategy for checking mathematical computation answers.

   123 + 456/579

   First add the digits 1 + 2 + 3 = 6; then add 4 + 5 + 6 = 15. Add 1 + 5 = 6. (Keep adding the digits until you get down to a one-digit number.) Take the two sums (6 and 6), add them, and you will get 12. These digits need to be added again: 1 + 2 = 3.

   Now take the sum from the original problem, 579, and add all the digits: 5 + 7 + 9 = 21. Add 2 + 1 = 3. If your top sum matches your bottom sum, your calculations are correct!

   Casting out nines simply means that you can throw out any nines or digits that add up to nine.

   For example, using the same problem, you can cast out two nines: the 4 and 5 because their sum is 9, and the number 9 in the sum. Follow the same procedure, but exclude those numbers casted out. 1 + 2 + 3 = 6; 6 is the only digit left in the other addend; add 6 + 6 = 12; add 1 + 2 = 3. Using the digits 5 + 7, add them to get 12; add 1 + 2 = 3. The sums match.

   123 + 456/579

5. Casting out nines with division requires an extra step. Using the problem 246 ÷ 6 = 41, 246 is the dividend, 6 is the divisor, and 41 is the quotient. Nines cannot be cast out, so add the digits of each: 246 = 2 + 4 + 6 = 12 = 1 + 2 = 3. In this case, 6 is the only digit for the divisor, and 41 = 4 + 1 = 5. Because division and multiplication are reverse operations, multiply the digit sums of the divisor (6) and the quotient (5): 6 × 5 = 30. Add the digits for 30 = 3 + 0 = 3. If that sum matches the digit sum of the dividend, the computation is correct.

$$\begin{array}{r} 41 = (4 + 1 = 5) \\ 6 \overline{\smash{)}246 = (2 + 4 + 6 = 12 = 1 + 2 = \underline{3})} \end{array}$$

Multiply divisor × quotient

6 × 5 = 30 = 3 + 0 = $\underline{3}$

Journaling: Present the students with two or three division problems that, when solved, will generate remainders. Ask the students to solve these problems using only words. (Students will also explain how to solve the problem in narrative form.)

2 × 2 = *Boo* (1995) by Loreen Leedy

(Grades 3–5) This comic book–style selection focuses on multiplication and has a Halloween theme. As with *Subtraction Action,* Leedy uses short chapters to illustrate different concepts, such as multiplying by 0 (The Disappearing Zero), multiplying by 1 (One More Time), and multiplying by 5 (Boo Stew). The author also includes the multiplication facts for 1–5.

Suggestions for Classroom Use

1. To assist students in developing a conceptual understanding of multiplication, have them demonstrate the multiplication facts using base-10 blocks. For example, 4 × 3 = 12 would be illustrated as:

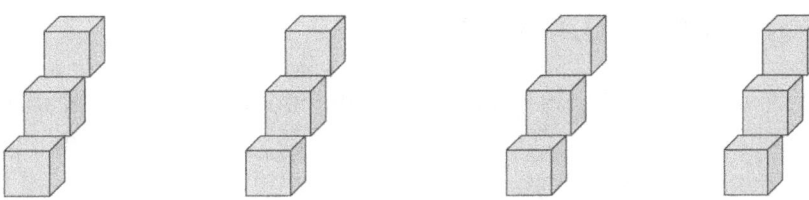

2. Students will enjoy generating their own multiplication story problems using Halloween as the theme. For example, three people came to the Halloween party dressed up as witches, and two people dressed up as ghosts. How many people dressed up as witches and ghosts? Show students how to develop questions based on the different types of multiplication and division questions (i.e., equal groups, combinations, area, and comparisons). Make sure students solve their problems and share them with their peers.

3. To help illustrate the commutative property of multiplication, have the students use counters to create arrays. Students will see the property in action, thus strengthening their conceptual understanding.

   $3 \times 2 = 6 \quad 2 \times 3 = 6$

 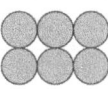

4. Students can use their creative minds to develop additional chapters for *2 × 2 = Boo*, focusing on the remaining basic multiplication facts.

5. *Pigs Go to Market: Halloween Fun with Math and Shopping,* by Amy Axelrod, is another book that uses a Halloween theme to focus on mathematics and can be used to complement *2 × 2 = Boo*. Multiplication problems can be generated from the Pig family's shopping spree to buy Halloween candy at the market.

Journaling: Encourage students to write about the following: What is your favorite Halloween candy? What does one bag of this candy cost? How about two bags? three bags? four and five bags?

Spaghetti and Meatballs for All! (1997) by Marilyn Burns

(Grades 3–6) Mr. and Mrs. Comfort decide to hold a family reunion and invite 32 people over for a spaghetti dinner. Mrs. Comfort rents tables and chairs for the big dinner and creates a seating arrangement. However, once the guests arrive, the tables and chairs are continuously rearranged until they finally find an arrangement that will allow all of the family members to sit down and eat spaghetti and meatballs.

Suggestions for Classroom Use

1. This selection can be used to emphasize the area model for multiplication. Ask the students to find the area of each of the table's arrangements. (Provide the length and width measurements of each table.)

2. Ask students to find the perimeter of each of the tables and the different arrangements. Ask them to determine when multiplication can be used to find the perimeter.

    Students can practice the area formula (length × width) by finding the area of other objects or rooms in the classroom or at home.

3. Ask students to cover small rectangular cut-outs with counters to create an array. Students will see the connection with the array counters and the area formula.

4. The National Library of Virtual Manipulatives has virtual geoboards and rubber bands that students can use to create rectangular shapes. Ask the students to determine the area of each of the rectangles they create.

Journaling: Encourage students to write about the following: Ask students to plan their own spaghetti-and-meatball dinner with members of their family. How many will they invite? How will they arrange the seating?

Fractions

Students can experience frustration when working with fractions because they can be construed from multiple perspectives: part-whole, measure, set, ratio, and division. Part-whole interpretations involve a whole being divided into different parts. Measure involves viewing fractions as linear measures, such as on a number line. Set interpretations involve a given number of objects, rather than a whole. Fractions can also represent ratios and indicate division of different sets (Cathcart et al., 209–216). Students need a variety of experiences that move beyond the traditional part-whole understanding of fractions.

The Wishing Club (2007) by Donna Jo Napoli

(Grades 3–6) When Petey and his brothers and sisters form a wishing club, they wish upon a star, but they do not get exactly what they wish for. Petey wishes for a dollar but gets only a quarter, while his brother Joey wishes for a cookie but gets only half of it. His sisters also get only a fraction of what they wish for. Next, they all decide to wish for a pig, but they have to figure out if the fractions they receive from their wishes equal a whole pig. They make their wishes, and, the next day, their parents buy them a pig, and they name him Corkscrew.

Suggestions for Classroom Use

1. Ask students to model the fractions used in the story (e.g., ½, ¼, and ⅛) with fraction circles or bars. Fraction circles and bars are concrete manipulatives used to represent the different fractions. Class sets include one whole and the fractions ½, ⅛, ¼ , 1/5, 1/6, ⅛, 1/10 and 1/12, in bright colors. Also, ask students to draw a picture that represents the fractions. This allows students to model the fractions both concretely and pictorially. A template for fraction circles

and bars is provided in the Appendix. These manipulatives can be copied on to stock paper and then cut out. You can use these manipulatives to model the different fractions.

2. Introduce addition of fractions with different denominators. Using fraction bars or circles, demonstrate how trading the manipulatives can be based on color. For example, ½ + ¼ cannot be added as is because they have different denominators (they are different colors; ½ is pink and ¼ is yellow). The ½ piece can be traded in for two ¼ pieces, thus changing the problem to ²⁄₄ + ¼. Now that the fractions have the same denominator (are the same color), they can be added.

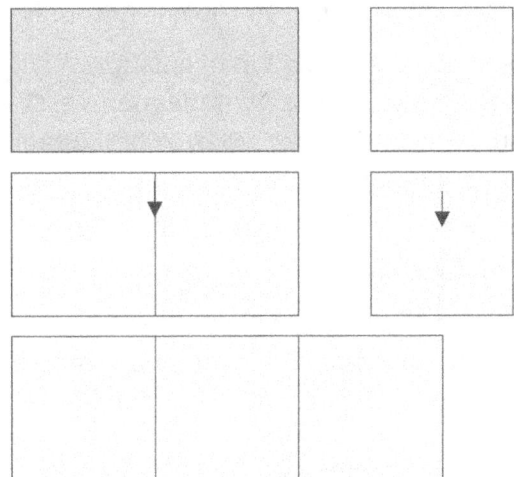

3. Students can work with Cuisenaire rods to develop an understanding of equivalent fractions and fraction sets. Cuisenaire rods are colored wooden rods of increasing length. These rods can be used to teach a variety of mathematical concepts, including fractions. The teacher or librarian can set a value for rods in one particular color, and the students will have to problem solve to figure out the fractional value of each of the other rods. These set values can change, since the rods are not assigned a specific value.

4. Ask students to imagine that Petey had additional siblings of different ages. Next, ask them to identify the portion of a wish these siblings would receive. Remind the students that their wishing fractions have to equal one whole.

5. Many students struggle with the concept of whole when working with fractions. Provide students with illustrations of the fractions used in the book. Using those illustrations, ask them to draw a picture of the whole.

Journaling: Encourage students to write about the following: Pretend you are a member of the wishing club. What would you wish for? What fraction of your wish would you receive?

Full House: An Invitation to Fractions (2007) by Dayle Ann Dodds

(Grades 3–6) Miss Bloom wants to fill five of the six rooms in the Strawberry Inn. As each guest checks in, fractions are used to indicate just how many rooms are occupied. For example, when Trainer P. Klein checks in, 4/6 of the rooms are filled. After all of the rooms are filled, Miss Bloom prepares a feast but forgets to serve the strawberry cake. When Miss Bloom occupies the sixth room the concept 6/6 = 1 is introduced. Throughout the book, pencil-and-watercolor illustrations depict a lively bunch, but, toward the end, five purple shadowy images are seen sneaking into the kitchen to devour the cake and reveal one final lesson: 6/6 of a strawberry cake can quickly be decreased to 1/6. The fractions are clearly written on each page and especially on the cake plate that suggests Miss Bloom will eat the final 1/6 of the cake.

Suggestions for Classroom Use

1. Ask the students to figure out the fractional value of rented rooms for each of the guests if Miss Bloom had 8 rooms in the house, 10 rooms, 12 rooms, and so on.

2. Fractions, decimals, and percents have a mathematical relationship. Ask students to figure out the decimal value and percent of each of the rooms that were rented. For example, when Salesman Jerome rented the third room, 3/6 or ½ of the rooms were full. The decimal value of ½ = .50, and the percent value is 50%.

3. Ask students to determine the fractional value of cake that the guests would receive if each one wanted two slice or three slices.

4. Allow students to design an actual floor plan of the Strawberry Inn. Samples of floor plans are offered on the Internet. Determine the common symbols that will be used for the floor plan, and identify what they will represent. This activity will give students practice with scale factors and ratios.

5. Students can generate a price list of what Miss Bloom charges for each room rental. Ask them to determine the amount Miss Bloom made with each visitor.

Journaling: Ask students to compare the prices of room rentals at different inns across the United States. Next, ask them to describe the inn they would like to visit. (Students can take virtual tours on the Internet.)

Piece = Part = Portion (2003) by Scott Gifford

(Grades 3–6) We use different words (e.g., hello) in different languages to express the same idea. We also use different words within the same language to express an idea. For example, a friendly greeting in English could be expressed with "Hello," "How do you do?," or "Hi." So it is with fractions, decimals, and percents. The author explains that these words all describe the same thing: a part of something. The point is further cemented by the double-page spreads that follow. Each one includes a written fraction, percent, and decimal opposite a rich complementary photograph. For example, 1/10 of your toes is followed by .10 and 10%, while the illustration shows two feet with one big toe sticking out of the hole in the sock of the left foot. Some of the fractions are not exact, for example, 1/8 and 1/7, and, after a brief explanation of how to find the decimal and percent version of a fraction, readers have to figure out how 1/5 of a pack of gum is .20 and 20% of a pack, on their own or with the help of a teacher or a teacher-librarian.

Suggestions for Classroom Use

1. To demonstrate their conceptual understanding of the value of fractions, students can draw illustrations depicting different fractions.

2. For each of their illustrations, ask students to identify the decimal and percent value.

3. Bring in shopping ads from the local newspaper that show a sale, such as 30% off of different items, and ask students to determine the new value of the item. This can be done with a grocery store ad, as well. Consider allowing students to use coupons, too.

4. Using pattern blocks, identify one whole of different shapes. Ask the students to determine the fractional value of the other pattern shapes. For example, three hexagons can equal a whole. What fraction and percentage is the triangle? Rhombus? A template for pattern blocks is provided in the Appendix. Again, these manipulatives can be copied on to stock paper, and then cut out. Pattern blocks can be used to represent different fractions. Teachers and librarians can identify a whole (1) with the blocks and have students figure out the value of the other blocks.

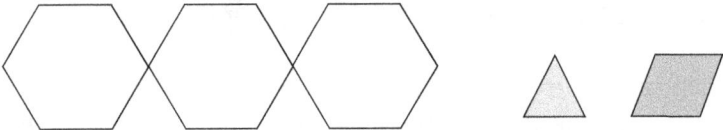

5. Students will enjoy creating illustrations or taking photographs to represent different fractions, ratios, and percents as the author did in this literature selection.

Journaling: Ask the students to explain the difference between part-whole models of fractions and part of a set model of fractions.

The Doorbell Rang (1986) by Pat Hutchins

(Grades K–5) Ma has made plenty of cookies for Victoria and Sam, who divide them so that they each have six. While they compare the cookies to their memory of the ones Grandma always bakes, the doorbell rings, and two neighbors are invited in to share the cookies, too. Each time the doorbell rings, the cookies are divided (and compared to Grandma's) until there are only enough cookies for each child to have one. When the bell rings for the last time, it is Grandma, and she is carrying a large tray of cookies.

Suggestions for Classroom Use

1. Allow the students to act out this story. As the doorbell rings and new friends arrive, ask students to determine the fractional value of the cookies left.

2. Ask the students to determine the fractional value of cookies left with different quantities as the whole.

3. Students can generate subtraction equations to represent the number of cookies being given to Victoria and Sam's friends.

4. Provide students with illustrations of cookies that represent different fractions, and ask them to determine the whole. For example, represents half of the total cookies. How many whole cookies are there?

5. Provide students with different fractional values, and ask them to compare the fractions by drawing pictures of cookies using 12 as the whole.

Journaling: Encourage students to investigate different recipes for making chocolate chip cookies. What fractional values of the different ingredients are needed to make them?

Centipede's 100 Shoes (2002) by Tony Ross

(Grades 2–5) A centipede hurts his toe and decides to get 100 shoes—50 left ones and 50 right ones. When he puts on his new shoes, he discovers he has 58 shoes left over and the shoes he is wearing hurt his feet. His aunts knit him some socks, but putting on all of the socks and shoes is a bother, so he gives them to his spider, beetle, woodlice, grasshopper, and worm friends.

Suggestions for Classroom Use

1. Using 100 shoes as the whole, provide the students with the following information: ½ of the shoes are tennis shoes, ¼ of the shoes are sandals, and 2/8 are boots. Next, ask the students to determine the number of the different types of shoes. The fractional value of the different types of shoes can change in order to pose different problems for the students.

2. Teachers and librarians can also provide the students with other problem situations involving fractions, such as the centipede needed only 42 shoes. What fraction did he need of the 100 shoes that he bought? What fraction value of the shoes did he not need?

3. Students will enjoy figuring out the fraction of shoes needed by the spiders, beetles, woodlice, grasshopper, and worms.

4. Students can also figure out the fraction of socks needed for each of Centipede's friends. Remember that the fractional whole changes from 100 to 42.

5. Identify other insects, animals, or sea creatures (e.g., octopus and crab), and ask the students to figure out the fractions of shoes they would need.

Journaling: Encourage students to write about the following: Why do you suppose the centipede bought 100 shoes when he needed only 42?

Works Cited

Cathcart, W. George, Yvonne Pothier, James Vance, and Nadine Bezuk. *Learning Mathematics in Elementary and Middle Schools.* Upper Saddle River, NJ: Pearson, 2006.

National Council of Teachers of Mathematics. *Principles and Standards for School Mathematics.* Reston, VA: National Council of Teachers of Mathematics, 2000.

Reid, H. (1995) On Mathematics and Music. Available at http://www.woodpecker.com/writing/essays/math+music.html (accessed July 19, 2009).

Van De Walle, John, Karen Karp, and Jennifer Bay-Williams. *Elementary and Middle School Mathematics.* Boston: Allyn and Bacon, 2010.

Children's Books Cited

Axelrod, Amy. *Pigs Go to the Market: Halloween Fun with Math and Shopping.* Illus. Sharon McGinley-Nally. New York: Aladdin, 1999.

Burns, Marilyn. *Spaghetti and Meatballs for All.* Illus. Debbie Tilley. New York: Scholastic, 1997.

Coats, Lucy. *Neil's Numberless World.* Illus. Neal Layton. New York: Dorling Kindersley, 2000.

Dodds, Dayle Anne. *Full House.* Illus. Abby Carter. Cambridge, MA: Candlewick Press, 2007.

Ehlert, Lois. *Fish Eyes: A Book You Can Count On.* New York: Harcourt Brace and Company.

Gifford, Scott. *Piece = Part = Portion.* Illus. Shmuel Thaler. Berkeley, CA: Tricycle, 2003.

Greenstein, Elaine. *Dreaming: A Countdown to Sleep.* New York: Arthur A. Levine, 2000.

Hamm, Diane Johnston. *How Many Feet in the Bed?* Illus. Kate Salley Palmer. New York: Aladdin, 1991.

Huck, Charlotte. *A Creepy Countdown.* Illus. Jos. A. Smith. New York: Greenwillow, 1998.

Hutchins, Pat. *The Doorbell Rang.* New York: Mulberry, 1986.

Leedy, Loreen. *Subtraction Action.* New York: Holiday House, 2000.

———. *Mission: Addition.* New York: Holiday House, 1997.

———. *2 × 2 = Boo.* New York: Holiday House, 1995.

McGrath, Barbara Barbieri. *The M&M's Count to One Hundred Book.* Watertown, MA: Charlesbridge, 2003.

Napoli, Donna Jo. *The Wishing Club.* Illus. Anna Currey. New York: Henry Holt, 2007.

Neuschwander, Cindy. *Amanda Bean's Amazing Dream.* Illus. Liza Woodruff. New York: Scholastic, 1998.

Pallotta, Jerry. *The Hershey's Kisses Addition Book.* Illus. Rob Bolster. New York: Scholastic, 2001.

———. *The Hershey's Kisses Subtraction Book.* Illus. Rob Bolster. New York: Scholastic, 2002.

Pinczes, Elinor J. *One Hundred Hungry Ants.* Illus. Bonnie Mackain. New York: Houghton Mifflin, 1993.

———. *A Remainder of One.* Illus. Bonnie Mackain. New York: Houghton Mifflin, 1995.

Ross, Tony. *Centipede's 100 Shoes.* New York: Henry Holt, 2002.

Tang, Greg. *The Best of Times*. Illus. Harry Briggs. New York: Scholastic, 2003.

———. *The Grapes of Math*. Illus. Harry Briggs. New York: Scholastic, 2001.

———. *Math Appeal*. Illus. Harry Briggs. New York: Scholastic, 2003.

———. *Math Fables*. Illus. Heather Cahoon. New York: Scholastic, 2001.

———. *Math Fables Too*. Illus. Taia Morley. New York: Scholastic, 2007.

———. *Math for All Seasons*. Illus. Harry Briggs. New York: Scholastic, 2005.

———. *Math Potatoes*. Illus. Harry Briggs. New York: Scholastic, 2005.

———. *Math-terpieces*. Illus. Greg Paprocki. New York: Scholastic, 2003.

Toft, Kim Michelle, and Allan Sheather. *One Less Fish*. Illus. Kim Michelle Toft. Watertown, MA: Charlesbridge, 1998.

Wood, Audrey. *The Napping House*. Illus. Don Wood. New York, Harcourt Brace and Company, 1984.

Zimelman, Nathan. *How the Second Grade Got $8,205.50 to Visit the Statue of Liberty*. Illus. Bill Slavin. Illinois: Albert Whitman, 1992.

Additional Titles

Adler, David A. *Fraction Fun*. Illus. Nancy Tobin. New York: Holiday House, 1996. (Grades 2–4)

>Readers are introduced to fractions with hands-on activities, such as using paper plates to illustrate and compare fractions, weighing coins and other objects, and graphing to discern equivalent fractions.

———. *Fun with Roman Numerals*. Illus. Edward Miller. New York: Holiday House, 2008. (Grades 2–5)

>Roman numerals are used on clocks, watches, buildings, and tombstones, but few youth know how to read or write them. This book offers simple instructions on how to read and write Roman numerals. First, Adler provides a review of the basic number system. Then he explains easy-to-follow hands-on activities that make practicing using Roman numerals fun.

———. *Working with Fractions*. Illus. Edward Miller. New York: Holiday House, 2007. (Grades 3–5)

>Illustrating that fractions are a part of daily life, the author shows various ways fractions can be used to describe the activities at a birthday party: 5/7 of the partygoers find chairs during musical chairs, 3/10 of the balloons are red, and 2/8 of the pizza is eaten. The cartoon illustrations depict colorful characters, a clown and a magician, who work together to explain numerator, denominator, equivalent fractions, addition, subtraction, and multiplication.

Anno, Mitsumasa. *Anno's Magic Seeds*. New York: Philomel, 1995. (Grades K–3)

>A wizard gives Jack two golden seeds. Jack eats one, and he does not get hungry again until the following year. Following the advice of the wizard, he buries the other seed. The seed produces a plant that has two more seeds. Jack eats one seed and buries the other for several

years until he decides not to eat one of the seeds. Instead, he buries both seeds. Before long, Jack discovers how to quickly multiply the seeds. Also see *Anno's Mysterious Multiplying Jar* (1983).

Bang, Molly. *Ten, Nine, Eight.* New York: HarperCollins, 1983. (Grades K–1)

A little girl and her father count from 10 to 1 at bedtime, using objects all around them. Warm illustrations depict objects such as nine soft quiet friends, seven empty shoes, five round buttons, three kisses, and two arms hugging a fuzzy bear.

Base, Graeme. *Uno's Garden.* New York: Abrams, 2006. (Grades 2–5)

When Uno arrives in the forest, there are 10 Moopaloops, 100 plants, 0 buildings, and 1 Snortlepig. As years go by, the number of buildings and people increases, while the number of plants and animals decreases. Eventually, Uno's descendants succeed at slowly redeveloping the area so that plants and animals can thrive. When the area is healthy, the illustrations are bright and colorful, but, when the area is overpopulated by people and buildings, the illustrations are dark and gloomy. A brief note at the end explains how to play the number games based on the animals, plants, and buildings referred to in the story.

Berry, Lynne. *Duck Dunks.* New York: Henry Holt, 2008. (Grade K)

There is much to count in this rhyming text that describes the adventures of five busy ducks that spend the day at the beach swimming, diving, and splashing.

Bowen, Betsy. *Gathering: A Northwoods Counting Book.* Boston: Little, Brown, 1995. (Grades K–4)

In the spring, a family begins to prepare for winter, a time of year when temperatures will drop to 0 degrees. The wood block prints show the family planting crops, preserving fruit and fish, and gathering wood. The story progresses from 0 to 12 and from May to December, as indicated by the numeral and number word on the left-hand page and the name of the month printed on the bottom of the right-hand page.

Catalanotto, Peter. *Daisy 1, 2, 3.* New York: Simon and Schuster, 2003. (Grades K–1)

Mrs. Tuttle has 20 Dalmatians named Daisy in her obedience school, but she never gets confused because each Daisy is unique. Daisy 4 does four tricks, while Daisy 11 has 11 chew toys, and a double-page spread shows all of the Daisys from 1 to 20.

Cleary, Brian P. *The Action of Subtraction* (Math Is CATegorical). Illus. Brian Gable. Minneapolis, MN: Millbrook, 2006. (Grades K–4)

Rhyming text is used to describe what subtraction is and how it works.

Clements, Andrew. *A Million Dots.* Illus. Mike Reed. New York: Simon and Schuster, 2006. (Grades 1–4)

Beginning with 1, this book shows 1 million dots while introducing facts such as how many times a person blinks in a week and the number of pennies that would fill 22 one-gallon milk jugs.

Dobson, Christina. *Pizza Counting.* Illus. Matthew Holmes. Watertown, MA: Charlesbridge, 2003. (Grades K–4)

This book introduces basic counting, addition, and fractions. Each page shows how the blank cheese pizza in the shape of a 0 is filled with several types of toppings. For example, one pizza uses 9 pieces of green pepper, 10 meatballs, 11 strips of onion, and 12 salami slices to form the face of a clock. Four addition problems are staggered around the pizza. Other pizza art show a whale, a triceratops, and a four-leaf clover. Facts about how pizzas have been made over the years, how they are prepared in Italy, and how long it takes to cook a pizza are informative, but the pizza chart at the end will really help readers visualize the fractions.

Dodds, Dayle Ann. *The Great Divide.* Illus. Tracy Mitchell. Cambridge, MA: Candlewick, 1999. (Grades 1–4)

When 80 people begin the cross-country race called The Great Divide, they have no idea of the obstacles they will face. The group separates as it gets closer to a canyon, and before they can go further, the group has dwindled to 40 people. The number of racers continues to decrease due to choices the racers make and unforeseen mishaps.

———. *Minnie's Diner: A Multiplying Menu.* Illus. John Manders. Cambridge, MA: Candlewick, 2004. (Grade K–2)

The five McFay boys and their Papa have lots of chores to do, but one by one they abandon them to go down to Minnie's Diner. The smallest son goes to the diner first and orders one special, while each brother follows, demanding that Minnie gives him an order twice as big as the one the brother before him enjoyed. By the time Papa McFay enters the diner, Minnie has served his biggest son 16 dishes of soup, salads, sandwiches, fries, and cherry pies, and Minnie knows Papa McFay is going to ask for double, too. The gouache illustrations show a hurried Minnie and clear, countable dishes of food.

Duke, Kate. *Twenty Is Too Many.* New York: Dutton, 2000. (Grades K–2)

When the book opens, 1 lone guinea pig sits playing checkers, but, by the end of the book, there are 10 guinea pigs that are so exhausted from playing that 10 moms and dads have to soothe them with hugs. As the number of dancing and singing guinea pigs increases, the number of objects on the page does, too. There are large, colorful numbers, plus signs, and equal signs in the center of the page, while complete equations appear in the bottom corner of the right-hand page. Also see Duke's counting book, *One Guinea Pig Is Not Enough* (1998).

Edwards, Pamela Duncan. *Roar: A Noisy Counting Book.* Illus. Henry Cole. New York: HarperCollins, 2000. (Grades K–2)

A lion cub looks for friends among jungle animals such as a red monkey, two flamingos, and eight gazelles, but when he roars they run away. He eventually runs into nine lion cubs and feels happy and accepted, loud roar and all. Some might frown at the suggestion that happiness and acceptance come only when the cub finds animals that look like he does.

Ekeland, Ivar. *The Cat in Numberland.* Illus. John O'Brien. Chicago, IL: Cricket, 2006. (Grades 3–5)

The numbers in Numberland live in Hotel Infinity in their respective room numbers. For leisure, they play four games: addition, subtraction, multiplication, and addition. When zero comes to the hotel looking for a room, its owners, Mr. and Mrs. Hilbert, disagree about whether zero is a number, but finally Mr. Hilbert is convinced, and the couple discovers a way to make room for zero. Zero causes even more trouble when he introduces his friends, 26 letters, to the other numbers. They all make equations. When foreigners called fractions want to move in, more trouble brews because the Hilberts do not know how to fit the fractions into the hotel because there are so many of them, but zero shows them how to make everyone fit. Each time the numbers change rooms to make room for others, the family cat becomes confused, until one day she leaves Numberland for good.

Engels, Christiane. *Knick-knack Paddy Whack.* Cambridge, MA: Barefoot, 2008. (Grades K–3)

Acrylic and digital collage illustrations contemporize the folk song "This Old Man." The children play instruments and dance through the streets while small, colorful numbers are scattered on the double-page spreads. A CD, lyrics, and sheet music make using the song to learn counting easy.

Fisher, Doris. *One Odd Day.* Illus. Karen Lee. Mount Pleasant, SC: Sylvan Dell, 2006. (Grades K–2)

When the alarm clock sounds, a boy wakes up and notices that all of the numbers on his clock are odd. Partially dressed, he can find only one sock and one shoe, and he is surprised to see his shirt has three sleeves. Things really seem strange when his dog has five legs and October is filled with odd numbers. He starts to relax when his math teacher explains that odd and even numbers exist, and when he wakes up the next morning his dog has four legs and his shoes and socks come in pairs again, but his mother has two heads. The "Creative Minds" section at the end of the book extends the focus on odd numbers.

Fisher, Valorie. *How High Can a Dinosaur Count?: And Other Math Mysteries.* New York: Schwartz and Wade, 2006. (Grades 1–4)

The 15 problems featured in this book encourage readers to use counting, addition, subtraction, and estimation. The problems featured on the left are poetic and filled with interesting characters such as Heloise, who wants to buy all of the hats in Madame Millie's Millinery but cannot afford them all, and Dixie's dad, who shares most of his 12 balloons with neighbors. A complementary illustration follows each problem, and answers (and additional questions) to all of the problems are in the back of the book.

Friedman, Aileen. *The King's Commissioners* (A Marilyn Burns Brainy Day Book). Illus. Susan Guevara. New York: Scholastic, 1994. (Grades 2–4)

Whenever the king has a problem in his kingdom, he appoints a commissioner to solve it. Now he has lost track of the number of commissioners who work for him. Determined to keep better records, he decides he and his royal advisers will count them. One adviser counts by twos and another by fives, causing the king to challenge the validity of their arithmetic. After a while, the king's daughter helps her father see that there are several valid ways to count the commissioners. An extensive note to adults explains the concepts, how children learn math, and how to discuss the math featured in the book.

Fromental, Jean-Luc. *365 Penguins.* Illus. Joelle Jolivet. New York: Harry N. Abrams, 2006. (Grades K–4)

On the first day of the year, a family receives a single penguin and an unsigned note that suggests other penguins will follow. When they do, the family uses math to make sense of how to house and feed them. The family tries to organize them in groups, count them, and measure their food. After the family receives 365 penguins, Uncle Victor, an ecologist, arrives and explains that he sent the penguins to try to protect them. The family waves good-bye to Uncle Victor and is relieved that he has left only one penguin behind.

Giganti, Paul. *Each Orange Had 8 Slices: A Counting Book.* New York: Greenwillow, 1992. (Grades K–3)

Specific questions about each gouache illustration encourage counting, adding, and multiplying flower petals, ants, wheels, balloons, orange slices, eggs, and so on. Also see *Counting Many Ways* (2002) and *How Many Blue Birds Flew Away?: A Counting Book with a Difference* (2005).

Giogas, Valarie. *In My Backyard.* Illus. Katherine Zecca. Mt. Pleasant, SC: Sylvan Dell, 2007. (Grades K–3)

From a distance, a nameless male protagonist watches 10 types of wildlife in his backyard. Animals like porcupines, squirrels, raccoons, and bunnies are gazing, spying, squinting, slithering, and sleeping near the boy. Rhyming couplets introduce words for groups of different types of wildlife: nursery of cubs, nest of bunnies, pit of hatchlings, and skulk of pups. Some of the illustrations are dark and shadowy, making some of the animals difficult to count, but the colorful list identifying each animal featured in the "For Creative Minds" section in the back of the book makes counting easier. "For Creative Minds" also includes facts about the animals presented; signs (droppings, nests, tracks) that animals leave to indicate they are around; tips for caring for wildlife; and suggestions for helping injured wildlife.

Goldstone, Bruce. *Great Estimations.* New York: Henry Holt, 2006. (Grades 1–4)

This book offers helpful strategies to help readers make sound estimations. The first strategy involves eye training, looking at several amounts of the same item and estimating the number of a third amount. For example, one can train the eye to see the difference between 100 pieces of elbow macaroni and 500 elbows by looking at a picture of both. Next, the author shows a larger amount of elbows, and the reader must estimate how many elbows are shown. Another strategy is called clump counting, counting 10 of the items in a large group and then counting the rest by observing the amount of space 10 items occupy. Box and count takes place when one divides a group of objects into 100 boxes, counts the things in one of the boxes, and then multiplies the number of items by 100 to determine the estimate. Also see Goldstone's follow-up, *Greater Estimations* (2008).

Hoban, Tana. *Let's Count.* New York: Greenwillow, 1999. (Grades K–2)

Photographs show familiar objects, such as chickens, eggs, wheels, tissues, and cherries, that can be counted from 1 to 100. Each left-hand page has a large numeral, the number word, and an equal number of dots. Other books by Hoban are *Count and See* (1972), *26 Letters and 99 Cents* (1987), and *More, Fewer, Less* (1998).

Hong, Lily Toy. *Two of Everything: A Chinese Folktale.* Morton Grove, IL: Albert Whitman, 1993. (Grades K–4)

One morning, Mr. Haktak, a poor farmer, finds a pot. The pot is so large he decides to put his purse inside it and carry it home. When Mrs. Haktak sees the pot, she leans over it to try to determine what they should do with it. While she is leaning over, her hairpin falls in; she reaches in to get it and pulls out two hairpins and two purses with coins. She quickly surmises that if they put the purses filled with coins back inside the pot, the coins will multiply. The airbrushed acrylic and gouache illustrations show money and objects multiplying quickly. One day, Mr. Haktak and Mrs. Haktak fall into the pot, and two of each crawl out. The original couple decide to take the new couple on as friends and next-door neighbors.

Hulme, Joy N. *Sea Sums*. Illus. Carol Schwartz. New York: Hyperion, 1996. (Grades K–2)

Sea animals are used as the subject of addition and subtraction problems that are written in numerical form at the bottom of the page. The animals featured are described in the back of the book. A similar book by Hulme, *Sea Squares* (1993), focuses on counting and multiplication.

Hutchins, Pat. *Ten Red Apples*. New York: Greenwillow, 2000. (Grades K–2)

The endpapers show a farmer and his wife counting from 1 to 10 and then from 10 to 1, introducing the counting down featured in the rhyming story. The farmer's tree has 10 apples on it, but each of his animals, from the horse to the hen, take 1, leaving only 1 for him. When he comes to the tree, all of the apples are gone, but it is not long before the farmer spots another tree filled with apples. The farmer's wife intends to use them all to bake a pie. The brightly colored illustrations are accompanied by a flowered border that is great for encouraging children to count just a little beyond 10.

Johnson, Stephen T. *City by Numbers*. New York: Penguin, 1999. (Grades K–5)

Numbers from 1 to 21 are shown against the urban backdrop of skyscrapers, fire escapes, garbage cans, sidewalks, and so on.

Katz, Karen. *Ten Tiny Tickles*. New York: Simon and Schuster, 2005. (Grade K)

Mom wakes baby with numerous tickles. As each tickle is counted, readers can count the equivalent number of daisies. Available in hardcover and in a board book, the book also emphasizes parts of the body.

Kunhardt, Katharine. *Let's Count the Puppies*. New York: HarperCollins, 2004. (Grade K–1)

Labrador retrievers are counted from 1 to 12 while they do several activities such as stare into the camera, snuggle in a wreath, huddle in a kettle, and bathe in the bathtub.

Lee, Cora, and Gillian O'Reilly. *The Great Number Rumble*. Illus. Virginia Gray. Toronto: Annick, 2007. (Grades 4–8)

Jeremy's best friend, Sam, is a "mathnik" who sees the importance of math all around him. When the Director of Education says the schools' curriculum will exclude math, everyone is happy except Sam, inciting the Number Rumble. Sam sets out to show the community that math permeates the world. Using experiences (e.g., cycling, gaming, skateboarding) that are important to adolescents, Sam convinces everyone that math must stay in the curriculum. Some informative sidebars feature biographies of mathematicians such as Pythagoras, Archimedes, and Charles Lutwidge Dodgson, while others surround Jeremy's attempt to make sense of what he is learning from Sam about probability, Fibonacci numbers, superstring theory, palindrome numbers, and so on. A rich glossary and recommendations for further reading are appended.

Lee, Huy Voun. *One, Two, Three, Go!* New York: Henry Holt, 2000. (Grades K–1)

Lee uses cut-paper collage to create illustrations that depict active children, numbering 1–10, who swim, pull, tiptoe, and jump, introducing readers to counting and Chinese writing.

Leedy, Loreen. *Missing Math: A Number Mystery.* New York: Marshall Cavendish, 2008. (Grades K–2)

When a town's numbers disappear, its citizens begin to have problems. Students cannot study math in school, and people cannot play sports or turn to their favorite television channels. Money no longer has value, and mail cannot be sent. The illustrations show animals trying to use items that usually display numbers. For example, a puppy will not eat the food his dad prepared because the numbers in the cookbook were missing, and a hippopotamus dressed in a bathrobe gets on a scale, but question marks appear where her weight should be. A detective finally discovers who stole the town's numbers by tracking a raccoon that plans to use the numbers to reach infinity. Definitions of words such as "quantity," "calculate," and "infinity" are featured amid the action on select pages.

———. *Fraction Action.* New York: Holiday House, 1994. (Grades K–2)

In three of the sections in the book, Miss Prime is teaching her students about fractions. After drawing a circle on a transparency and illustrating one-half, she encourages the students to think about fractions they encounter daily. Speech and thought bubbles reveal images of a tuna sandwich cut in half, half a glass of juice, a half-full piggy bank, and so on, before Miss Prime introduces the concepts of one-third and one-fourth and asks the students to imagine again. As Miss Prime continues her lesson, she puts the students in groups and gives them manipulatives like marbles. One section is devoted to using fractions to divide food among friends at Sadie's house, and another introduces the use of fractions at Tally's lemonade sell. The final section goes back to Miss Prime's class, where a test on fractions is given. Throughout the book, there are questions related to fractions, and the answers are at the end of the book.

Long, Lynette. *Dealing with Addition.* Watertown, MA: Charlesbridge, 1998. (Grades 1–3)

Long begins by explaining the basics of the card deck, from the description of the symbols to the names of specific cards. She then explains the numerous ways cards can be sorted (e.g., by color, number, face). Finally, she shows how the numbers and symbols on the cards can be added together. The book ends with step-by-step directions for playing "Dealing with Addition." Also see *Domino Addition* (1996).

MacDonald, Suse. *Fish, Swish! Splash, Dash!: Counting Round and Round.* New York: Little Simon, 2007. (Grades K–2)

Die-cut pages reveal colorful fish that readers can count from 1 to 10; flip the book, and count down from 10 to 1.

———. *Look Whooo's Counting.* New York: Scholastic, 2000. (Grade K)

A wise owl teaches herself to count the 10 types of animals she sees at night. The illustrator uses dark colors and clever strategies to help reinforce the numbers. For example, the three ducks' wings form the number 3 and the owl's wings seem to form numbers 1, 2, and 3 on one double-page spread.

McMillan, Bruce. *Eating Fractions*. New York: Scholastic, 1991. (Grade K–2)

Photographs of food depict whole, halves, thirds, and fourths in this virtually wordless picture book. Each food is shown in its whole form before revealing a portion of it. For example, the book begins with two children looking happily at a whole banana, while the next single page spread shows the hands of an adult male cutting the banana in half. The children spend the day eating muffins, pizza, corn, pear salad, and strawberry pie. Before each food is shared, it is cut into halves, thirds, or fourths so that the concepts are repeated throughout the book. The numerals and numbers words are shown so that underneath a whole strawberry pie is the word "whole" and a small number one, while the opposite page shows a little girl cutting the pie as her eager friend stands near her with his plate. The next page shows the girl cutting the pie in fourths; thus, the diagram beneath the photo shows a whole pie divided into four pieces and four images of a quarter of a pie. The author's recipes are appended, along with an author's note urging adults and children to cook and eat a math lesson. Also see *Jelly Beans for Sale* (1996).

Micklethwait, Lucy. *I Spy Two Eyes: Numbers in Art*. New York: Greenwillow, 1993. (Grades 1–2)

The author uses the "I Spy" game to encourage readers to count up to 20 different objects (e.g., 1 fly, 4 fish, 7 circles, 16 apples, and so on) in 19 medieval paintings and 1 woodblock print on each right-hand page. An "I Spy" phrase containing a number word and numeral is printed in large fonts on each left-hand page with the artist's name and the title of the painting printed below it. Works by artists such as Henri Matisse, Vincent Van Gogh, Thomas Cooper Gotch, and Pablo Picasso are reproduced against a white background. The book ends with additional information about each work of art.

Mills, Claudia. *7 × 9 = Trouble!* Illus. Brain G. Karas. New York: Farrar, Straus and Giroux, 2004. (Grades 2–3)

Third-grader Wilson Williams is having a difficult time learning the 12 multiplication tables, but his family and friends help, making it possible for him to earn an ice cream cone from his teacher.

Murphy, Stuart J. *Jump, Kangaroo, Jump!* (Math Start). Illus. Kevin O'Malley. New York: HarperCollins, 1998. (Grades 2–3)

It is field day, and Kangaroo and all his 11 Australian friends are excited. The first game they play is tug-of-war, so the counselor, Ruby, tells the campers to split in halves. Before the campers participate in the swimming relay race, Ruby asks them to form three teams so each team will have one-third of the campers. Next, the campers form four teams that compete in a canoe race. Though Kangaroo is on a winning team during some of the events, it is the last event that really allows him to shine, as each camper competes to see who can win the long jump. A note to adults and children offer sample questions and activities.

———. *Give Me Half* (Math Start). Illus. G. Brian Karas. New York: HarperCollins, 1996. (Grades 1–3)

In this rhyming story, a brother and sister reluctantly share pizza, juice, and cupcakes, introducing the concepts "half," "whole," and "division." The illustrations reveal two youngsters ready to protest the idea of splitting everything in half, everything except the responsibility of cleaning up the mess from their food fight. Appended is a note to adults and children about how to ingest and practice the concepts taught in the book.

Nagda, Ann Whitehead. *Cheetah Math: Learning about Division from Baby Cheetahs.* New York: Henry Holt, 2007. (Grade 3–5)

The right-hand pages in this book describe how two cheetahs, Majani and Kubali, are raised at the San Diego Zoo, while the pages on the left use the cubs' lives as a springboard for division lessons. Terms such as "division," "dividend," "divisor," and "quotient" are introduced first. Repeated subtraction is emphasized, and charts and graphs make the concepts clear. Division problems ask readers to figure out the amount of milk and meat the cubs eat, how fast they run and grow, and how many years might pass before cheetahs become extinct. The book's color photographs show the cubs with trainers, dog buddies, and zoo visitors. Nagda also wrote *Panda Math* (2005).

Nagda, Ann Whitehead, and Cindy Bickel. *Polar Bear Math: Learning about Fractions from Klondike and Snow.* New York: Henry Holt, 2004. (Grades 1–5)

This book follows the nurturing that two baby polar bears, Klondike and Snow, experienced at the Denver Zoo after Ulu, their mother, abandoned them. In between describing the care of the twin bears, the author presents lessons about fractions, explaining terms such as "numerator," "denominator," "common denominator," and "equivalent fractions." Fractions are also introduced in the recipe for polar bear milk, the amount of milk bottles the bears drink, and the time the zoo personnel devote to taking care of them. One fraction lesson focuses on how much time the bears spend at the zoo hospital and at the home of a member of the team devoted to taking care of them. Another fraction lesson compares Snow's weight to Klondike's. The graphs used are clear and helpful, and color photographs track the bears' development until they have their first birthday.

Napoli, Donna Jo, and Richard Tchen. *How Hungry Are You?* Illus. Amy Walrod. New York: Atheneum, 2001. (Grades K–2)

Two friends, a rabbit and a frog, decide to have a picnic, but they have just enough food (12 sandwiches and a jug of bug juice) for the two of them. On their way to the park, they meet several friends who want to join them, and they soon discover that dividing the food among 13 friends is complicated. Cut-paper illustrations show all of the friends sharing the food they contributed to what has become a party. Small pictures of each animal followed by the words they say helps readers distinguish between the speakers.

O'Sullivan, Robyn. *Your 206 Bones, 32 Teeth, and Other Body Math* (National Geographic Science Chapters). Washington, DC: National Geographic, 2006. (Grades 1–4)

This book illustrates how numbers are often used to discuss the human body and all of its parts, from the more than 75 trillion cells in an adult to the 300 bones in a newborn's body. Readers learn that bodies have more than 200 joints, more than 600 muscles, and more than 100,000 hairs. Color photographs throughout show diverse children at play. A final chapter encourages readers to measure how fast their bodies can perform, while tips on writing reports and a helpful glossary conclude the book.

Packard, Edward. *Big Numbers: And Pictures That Show Just How Big They Are!* Illus. Sal Murdocca. Brookfield, Connecticut: Millbrook, 2000. (Grades 1–2)

When the book begins, a boy, a dog, and a cat observe a single pea on a plate. The peas grow in number exponentially, from 10, to 100, to 1,000, on up to a million, a billion, and a trillion, and burst out of the house and eventually flood the community. The book concludes with a definition of infinity and an author's note about his strategy for determining the number of peas it would take to fill a house. Comic book panels, speech bubbles, zany factoids, and an ever-growing number of peas add humor to the story. Packard also wrote *Little Numbers: And Pictures That Show Just How Little They Are* (2001).

Pallotta, Jerry. *Apple Fractions.* Illus. Rob Bolster. New York: Scholastic, 2002. (Grades K–3)

Science and math combine in this book about apples and fractions. Elves demonstrate one-half, three-thirds, one-third, and two-thirds by cutting different types of apples. Terms such as "denominator," "numerator," and "whole numbers" are introduced alongside words like "stem," "pulp," and "core."

———. *The Hershey's Milk Chocolate Bar Fractions Book.* Illus. Rob Bolster. New York: Scholastic, 1999. (Grades 1–4)

Hershey's milk chocolate bars illustrate fractions. For example, equivalent fractions are shown by positioning each half of a chocolate bar on a page and showing that 6/12 equals ½. The next page introduces ⅓ and begins to explain how to add, subtract, and divide fractions. In between lessons using a chocolate bar are pages that reinforce skills taught. The concept of ⅛ is introduced while sharing information about cocoa pods. Also see *The Hershey's Kisses Addition Book* (2001).

———. *Ocean Counting: Odd Numbers.* Illus. Shennen Bersani. Watertown, MA: Charlesbridge, 2005. (Grades 2–4)

A companion book for *Underwater Counting: Even Numbers* (2001), this book introduces facts about more sea creatures. Beginning with 1 striped bass to 49 smelts (50 and 0 are thrown in at the end to introduce even numbers), readers practice counting with odd numbers. Colored-pencil illustrations reveal the details of beautiful creatures, like 5 blood stars, 11 northern stars, and 45 whelks.

———. *Underwater Counting: Even Numbers.* Illus. David Biedrzycki. Watertown, MA: Charlesbridge, 2001. (Grades 3–5)

The first double-page spread reveals an image of an ocean done in Adobe Photoshop, but there are no sea creatures in the picture. Next, a single page shows one eel and gives a few details about the green moray eel, while the opposite page shows two coral groupers. From there, underwater animals are counted by even numbers up to 50. It is difficult to see the images of some of the animals, including the 16 parrotfish and the 40 bird-nose wrasses, well enough to count them. But most images are striking, such as the whale's eye and the 26 lice that surround it and the shapes and colors of the 4 clown triggerfish.

Pinczes, Elinor J. *Arctic Fives Arrive.* Illus. Holly Berry. Boston: Houghton Mifflin, 1996. Grades K–2)

The hoots of five snowy owls awaken 5 bears, who decide they want to join them atop a hillcrest, making it necessary for the owls to count by 5s to determine if they can all fit on the mound. Before long, the owls and the bears must make room for other sets of 5—ermine, walrus, hares, oxen—until 30 animals sit enjoying the Northern Lights. Then, the counting goes from 30 to 0 as the groups of animals leave the mound.

———. *Inchworm and a Half.* Illus. Randall Enos. Boston: Houghton Mifflin, 2001. (Grades 1–3)

Inchworm measures all of the vegetables in the garden until one day she discovers she needs help measuring a cucumber because she needs an additional fraction, a one-half-inch worm. Together they go on to have fun in the garden measuring a radish and an asparagus spear until they discover they need help from a ⅛-inch worm and then a ¼-inch worm.

Schnitzlein, Danny. *The Monster Who Did My Math.* Illus. Bill Mayer. Atlanta, GA: Peachtree, 2007. (Grades 1–3)

A nameless boy who is terrified of mathematics, particularly addition, subtraction, and multiplication, needs help when he realizes it is Sunday night and his math homework is incomplete. When he feels all hope is lost, a frightening monster appears in his room and offers to do his math for a fee. While the boy signs a contract with the monster and defers payment, the monster sharpens his fingers and thumbs and begins the homework. On Monday, the boy gets an A+ on his homework, and he calls the monster for more help later that night. Once again he does well on his homework, but when his teacher tells him to work out a problem on the board, he is unsuccessful. Angry, he confronts the monster, who politely points out clause 93 of the contract, which explains that he is not responsible if the boy did not learn the mathematics concepts. In addition to that, the monster charges the boy $64 for his services. When he attempts to pay, the monster tells him he has miscounted. The boy scrambles to scrape up the balance, using math skills along the way. Rid of the monster, he begins his homework and slowly realizes math is not so bad.

Schwartz, David M. *On Beyond a Million: An Amazing Math Journey.* Illus. Paul Meisel. New York: Random House, 1999. (Grades 2–5)

Professor X and his dog, Y, have come to Bantam School to present at an assembly. When they arrive, the children are busy trying to stop a broken popcorn machine from flooding the school with kernels. Defeated, they decide to count the kernels. Since the process is taking a long time, Professor X decides to teach the students to count using exponentials. Speech bubbles and "Did You Know?" sidebars about various things, such as the United States population, the number of Tootsie Rolls made, and the weight of the Earth, are scattered throughout the book. Schwartz is also the author of *G Is for Googol: A Math Alphabet Book* (1998) and *If You Hopped Like a Frog* (1999).

Seeger, Laura Vaccaro. *One Boy.* New York: Roaring Brook, 2008. (Grades K–2)

One boy sits alone, painting pictures that feature various objects, making it easy for readers to count from 1 to 10. Readers will marvel at the three apes standing behind bars and at the ten lifelike ants crawling on a boy's stomach. The pages contain an open square, or die-cut, that reveals that shorter words are often in the middle of longer ones (e.g., "key" is a part of "monkey" and "car" is found in the word "carpet").

Shahan, Sherry. *Cool Cats Counting.* Illus. Paula Barragan. Little Rock, AR: August House, 2005. (Grades K–1)

Rhythmic text and dancing animals are used to teach numbers up to 10 in Spanish and English.

Shields, Carol Diggory. *Wombat Walkabout.* Illus. Sophie Blackall. New York: Dutton, 2009. (Grade K–2)

A glossary of words such as "walkabout," "kookaburra," and "swag" are presented before the rhyming story begins. Six wombats, all with distinct accessories like beads, hats, and hair bands, decide to take a walkabout, though they do not know that a dingo is watching them. As they walk around, each wombat becomes distracted by flowers, gum nuts, or pebbles and leaves the group. The dingo collects the wombats one by one until the last two, Jen and Jack, realizes what has happened and tries to save the others by digging a hole and luring the dingo into it. Successful, the wombats walk back home in pairs. Set in Australia, the illustrations show trees, rocks, and plants in green, brown, and tan.

Smith, Danna. *Two at the Zoo: A Counting Book.* Illus. by Valeria Petrone. New York: Clarion, 2009. (Grade K)

A little boy takes his grandfather to the zoo. Before going in, they purchase two red tickets. Once inside, they begin to count animals, from a black bear to 10 wart hogs. The rhyming text makes remembering the numbers easy, and the illustrations, rendered in digital gouache, are colorful and clear.

Stiegemeyer, Julie. *Gobble-Gobble Crash: A Barnyard Counting Bash.* Illus. Valeri Gorbachev. New York: Dutton, 2008. (Grades K–1)

Four rowdy turkeys disturb the peace in a country barn while their human neighbors and fellow animals (six chicks and eight goats, for example) try to rest.

Swinburne, Stephen R. *What's a Pair? What's a Dozen?* Honesdale, PA: Boyds Mills, 2000. (Grades K–1)

The author's foreword explains that numbers are an important part of life. Beginning with the number one, sparse text and vibrant color photographs introduce other number-related words: first, second, pair, triple, several, half dozen, and so on. One photograph shows a girl riding a unicycle on a hot summer day, and the text underneath defines the prefix uni-. Toward the end of the book, the reader's understanding of the concepts is put to the test, as questions are asked on one page and the answer is given on the back. Each page includes a photograph that helps the reader answer the question.

Thompson, Lauren. *One Riddle, One Answer.* Illus. Linda S. Wingerter. New York: Scholastic, 2001. (Grades 3–6)

Aziza, the daughter of a Persian sultan, tells her father she will use a riddle to help her select a husband. Any man in the land who can accurately answer each of the three parts of the riddle will be her husband. Many men try to answer the riddle and fail, but a farmer named Ahmed offers the correct answer. As he explains his rationale, he and Aziza fall in love. The book ends with a detailed explanation of how to solve the riddle.

Wells, Robert. *Can You Count to a Googol?* Morton Grove, IL: Albert Whitman, 2000. (Grades 2–4)

> Beginning with the number 10, the author shows how multiplication leads to larger numbers such as 100, 1,000, 100,000, and even a googol. Illustrations show what 10,000 pennies and 100,000 marshmallows might look like, while children stack and pack $1 million in a crate. An author's note explains how a number with 100 0s got its name, in the 1930s.

Williams, Brenda. *The Real Princess: A Mathemagical Tale.* Illus. Sophie Fatus. Cambridge, MA: Barefoot, 2008. (Grades 1–4)

> The king and queen are determined to help their three sons, Primo, Secundo, and Terzo, find a princess to marry. As each son falls in love, the queen places a golden pea underneath the woman's mattress to determine if she is really a princess and discovers that Terzo is the only one who really marries a princess. The illustrations are done in acrylics and collaged papers, and there is much to count in the tale: the number of servants, the number of bags of gold, the number of golden peas, and so on.

CHAPTER 4

Though some elementary school librarians and teachers might assume algebra should be introduced in middle school, the NCTM reports that experiences with algebra should begin in the early grades in order to lay the foundation for middle and upper grades (NCTM 37). Students in the lower elementary grades can work with simple patterns, both formally and informally, while, during the middle years, students can begin working with more sophisticated patterns, including the Fibonacci sequence (NCTM 38). To extend students' algebraic thinking, multiple representations of different mathematical ideas should be encouraged, including algorithms and formulas, graphs and tables, manipulatives, and oral explanations (NCTM 67–71). See Figure 4.1 for a list of books that encourage girls to have fun with algebra and more.

Algebra Expectations

The algebra standards maintain that students should be able to understand, describe, and continue patterns and functions (both linear and nonlinear) by sorting, classifying, and ordering objects. Students are expected to use algebraic symbols, understand numerical relationships, and analyze change and rates of change. Other expectations include the ability to use the different properties, to work with variables and equations through tables and graphs, to model problems, and to use representations (NCTM 90, 158, 222). The list of books in Figure 4.2 offers games and activities that can help students meet algebra expectations.

Using Mathematics Literature
The King's Chessboard (1988) by David Birch

(Grades 2–8) After a wise man serves the king, the king wants to give him a gift. The wise man tells the king a gift is not necessary, but the king insists. Feeling obligated to ask for a

Long, Lynette. *Math Smarts: Tips, Tricks, and Secrets for Making Math More Fun!* (American Girl Library Series). Illus. Tracy McGuinness. Middleton, WI: American Girl, 2004. (Grades 3–7)

McKellar, Danica. *Kiss My Math: Showing Pre-algebra Who's Boss.* New York: Hudson Street, 2008. (Grades 7–8)

———. *Math Doesn't Suck: How to Survive Middle School Math without Losing Your Mind or Breaking a Nail.* New York: Hudson Street, 2007. (Grades 6–8)

Wyatt, Valerie. *The Math Book for Girls and Other Beings Who Count.* Illus. Pat Cupples. Toronto: Kids Can, 2000. (Grades 3–6)

Figure 4.1 Girls and Mathematics

Anno, Mitsumasa. *Anno's Math Games II.* New York: Penguin, 1989. (Grades K–2)

Ball, Johnny. *Go Figure! A Totally Cool Book about Numbers.* New York: Dorling Kindersley, 2005. (Grade 4–8)

Blum, Raymond. *Mathamusements.* Illus. Jeff Sinclair. New York: Sterling, 1997. (Grades 4–6)

King, Andrew. *Math for Fun Projects* (Math for Fun). Brookfield, CT: Copper Beech, 1999. (Grades 2–4)

Long, Lynette. *Dazzling Division: Games and Activities That Make Math Easy and Fun* (Magical Math). New York: Wiley, 2000. (Grades 4–7)

———. *Fabulous Fractions: Games and Activities That Make Math Easy and Fun* (Magical Math). New York: Wiley, 2001. (Grades 3–6)

———. *Great Graphs and Sensational Statistics: Games and Activities That Make Math Easy and Fun* (Magical Math). New York: Wiley, 2004. (Grades 3–6)

Maganzini, Christy. *Cool Math: Math Tricks, Amazing Math Activities, Cool Calculations, Awesome Math Factoids and More.* Illus. Ruta Daugavietis. Los Angeles: Price Stern Sloan, 1997. (Grades 4–7)

Pappas, Theoni. *Adventures of Penrose the Mathematical Cat.* San Carlos, CA: Wide World Publishing/Tetra, 1997. (Grades 2–7)

Ross, Catherine Sheldrick. *Circles: Fun Ideas for Getting A-Round in Math.* Reading, MA: Addison-Wesley, 1993. (Grades 4–7)

Ross, Kathy. *Kathy Ross Crafts Triangles, Rectangles, Circles, and Squares* (Learning Is Fun!). Illus. Jan Barger. Brookfield, CT: Millbrook, 2002. (Grades K–1)

VanCleave, Janice Pratt. *Janice VanCleave's Geometry for Every Kid: Easy Activities That Make Learning Geometry Fun* (Science for Every Kid). New York: Wiley, 1994. (Grades 3–7)

———. *Janice VanCleave's Play and Find Out about Math: Easy Activities for Young Children* (Play and Find Out). New York: Wiley, 1997. (Grades K–1)

Zaslavsky, Claudia. *More Math Games and Activities from Around the World.* Chicago: Chicago Review, 2003. (Grades 3–7)

Figure 4.2 Math Games and Activities

gift, the man asks the king to place a grain of rice on the first square of a chessboard, two grains on the second, and four grains on the third and to continue to double the amount on each square until all 64 squares are full. The king agrees but has no idea how much rice he will need to fulfill the man's request. When he realizes that the village will run out of rice, he admits he cannot honor the man's request. This Indian folktale helps readers learn about exponential growth.

Suggestions for Classroom Use

1. Students will have fun working with a function machine. A function machine works like this:

   1. A number is put in (input).
   2. A rule is applied to the number.
   3. A number comes out (output).

   For example, the rule for each of the numbers used below is "Divide by 2."

   In 10, Out 5.

   In 14, Out 7.

   In 16, Out 8.

   In 20, Out 10.

   In 100, Out 50.

2. Ask students to complete a chart similar to a function machine. The input would be Day 1, Day 2 . . . Day 64. Students will need to determine the function rule and the output numbers.

3. Students can use manipulatives to create a visual representation of the growing number pattern. Multilink cubes can be used to show a pattern, and students can link cubes to continue the pattern. Multilink cubes are 2-cm plastic cubes. Each of them interlocks on all sides.

4. Ask the students to make a choice: Would they rather be given $1 million or for one month be given 1¢ the first day, 2¢ the second day, 4¢ the third day, and so on (following the pattern in *The King's Chessboard*). Ask students to determine the total amount they would receive if option 2 is chosen. Which choice is the best?

5. Ask students to explore different recipes that require rice and determine which day they would have enough rice to complete the recipe if they were the wise man. (Students may have to determine how many grains of rice are in a cup.)

6. *Anno's Magic Seeds* by Mitsumasa Anno can complement *The King's Chessboard*. This selection also focuses on number patterns, and things become a bit more complex as the story develops.

Journaling: Ask students to develop other number patterns showing exponential growth and exchange them with their peers so that they can determine the number rule used to create the pattern.

The Number Devil: A Mathematical Adventure (1997) by Hans Magnus Enzensberger

(Grades 6–8) Twelve-year-old Robert has been having nightmares, so he is surprised when one night he dreams he is in a meadow. While looking around the meadow, he notices a small old man who introduces himself as the number devil. Robert does not want to have anything to do with numbers or math, but the number devil visits repeatedly until Robert willingly tries to understand what the devil has to say about infinity, prime numbers, Fibonacci numbers, Pascal's triangle, and so on. The color illustrations, charts, and tables help clarify the concepts Robert is learning. A "Warning" in the back of the book explains that the number devil uses "unusual expressions" for mathematical concepts. For example, he calls prime numbers prima-donna numbers. The index helps readers get to specific topics of interest quickly.

Suggestions for Classroom Use

1. A number that is the same forward and backward is called a palindrome. Have students identify different palindromic dates (e.g., 20th of February, 2002 = 20, 02, 2002) or words (e.g., LEVEL).

2. Students will enjoy playing "Roman Numeral War." Students can create their own deck of cards, but they have to be written with roman numerals. Students can then play the traditional game of war. To play Roman Numeral War, arrange students in groups of two, three, or four. The dealer deals all cards face down. Each player draws one card, and the largest number wins. The player who has the largest number receives all the cards for that hand. The player with the most cards wins.

3. The Number Devil introduces Robert to the Sieve of Eratosthenes. This is an ancient algorithm for finding prime numbers. A Greek mathematician created this algorithm. Give students the opportunity to investigate the work of this famous mathematician.

   The National Library of Virtual Manipulatives includes a virtual activity that focuses on the Pythagorean Theorem. Students will enjoy this hands-on and visual approach to working with this theorem.

4. Lead students on a nature walk, and encourage them to look for Fibonacci's numbers in nature. For example, the flower black-eyed susans can have 13 petals, and shasta daisies can have 21 petals.

Journaling: The number devil uses many unconventional expressions for different mathematical terms. For example, he calls prime numbers prima-donna numbers and topological objects pretzels. Ask students to use their creativity to develop unusual terms for different mathematical terms. Inform the students that they must provide justification for their invented term.

The Adventures of Penrose the Mathematical Cat (1997) by Theoni Pappas

(Grades 6–8) When the author works on mathematics books, models, and papers, her cat, Penrose, always helps. Within each chapter filled with challenges and activities, Penrose is involved with different mathematical ideas, such as learning the truth about infinity and the mathematics of soap bubbles. The book focuses on many of the content standards, including Algebra, Geometry, and Numbers and Operations.

Suggestions for Classroom Use

1. Magic squares are mathematical puzzles of number patterns. When adding the columns and rows and each of the two corner numbers, the sums are the same. Usually the 3 × 3 magic square is the least complex magic square to solve. Ask students to complete their own magic squares.

8	1	6
3	5	7
4	9	2

Magic squares

2. Provide the students with a copy of Pascal's Triangle (Rows 0 through 7). Ask students to identify any patterns they might see and to complete the next few rows following the pattern. Elementary school students can color the even or odd numbers, prime numbers, or multiples of an identified number.

3. Fractals are shapes that are self-similar—that is, smaller aspects of the shape are similar in appearance to the larger or full shape. Show the students various illustrations of fractals before asking them to create their own. (Illustrations of fractals can be found on the Internet.) The Sierpinski Triangle can be used as an example.

Sierpinski Triangle

4. Students can make their own Chinese abacus. Introduce the abacus to the students, and demonstrate how it works. Directions for making an abacus can be found at <www.kidscrafts.com>.

5. Review squaring numbers ($5^2 = 5 \times 5 = 25$), and ask students to list the first 50 perfect squares.

Journaling: Encourage students to write about the following prompt: Take Penrose on a new mathematics adventure. Identify a concept that you would like to introduce Penrose to, and write a short story explaining this concept to the mathematical cat. Figure 4.3 has a list of math riddle books that students can use to find additional topics to write about.

Adler, David A. *Calculator Riddles*. Illus. Cynthia Fisher. New York: Holiday House, 1994. (Grades 3–6)

———. *You Can, Toucan, Math: Word Problem-Solving Fun*. Illus. Edward Miller. New York: Holiday House, 2007. (Grades 2–4)

Burns, Marilyn. *How Many Feet? How Many Tails?: A Book of Math Riddles* (Hello Reader!). Illus. Lynn Adams. New York: Scholastic, 1996. (Grades 1–2)

Holub, Joan. *Riddle-iculous Math*. Illus. Regan Dunnick. Morton Grove, IL: Albert Whitman. (Grades K–5)

Lewis, J. Patrick. *Arithme-Tickle: An Even Number of Odd Riddle-Rhymes*. Illus. Frank Remkiewicz. New York: Harcourt, 2002. (Grade 2–4)

Martin, Jannelle. *ABC Math Riddles: An ABC Riddles Book from Peel Productions* (ABC Riddles Series). Illus. Freddie Levin. Columbus, NC: Peel, 2003. (Grades 1–4)

McGrath, Barbara Barbieri. *Skittles Riddles Math*. Illus. Roger Glass. Watertown, MA: Charlesbridge, 2000. (Grades 1–3)

Tang, Greg. *The Grapes of Math: Mind-Stretching Math Riddles*. Illus. Harry Briggs. New York: Scholastic, 2001. (Grades 3–5)

———. *Math Appeal: Mind Stretching Math Riddles*. Illus. Harry Briggs. New York: Scholastic, 2003. (Grades 1–4)

———. *Math for All Seasons: Mind-Stretching Math Riddles*. Illus. Harry Briggs. New York: Scholastic, 2002. (Grades 1–3)

Figure 4.3 Math Riddles

Math Curse (1995) by Jon Scieszka and Lane Smith

(Grades 3–8) A young student believes that a math curse has been placed on him by Mrs. Fibonacci, his math teacher. Everywhere he looks and everything that he does seems to be related to math. One night he has a dream about fractions, and he breaks the math curse. Finally, he can work all of his math problems. This literary selection covers all of the mathematics content strands.

Suggestions for Classroom Use

1. The binary number system works only with two digits—0 and 1. Students will use their problem-solving skills when identifying the binary number for each of our decimal numbers. For example, 2 would be written as 10, and 3 would be written as 11.

2. Students will enjoy investigating the Mayan number system. Ask the students to develop a number chart using different symbols: a dot and a dash.

3. *Math Curse* is filled with interesting math questions and investigations. Ask students to solve the problems presented.

4. In this literature selection, the author presents true-false mathematical problems using money (e.g., 1 Washington = 25 Lincolns). Ask students to generate other mathematical problems in a similar fashion, exchange them with their peers, and solve them.

5. Ask students to write algebraic equations representing typical occurrences. For example, 24 hours per day for a year can be written 24×365.

Series Title	Publisher	Grade Level
Math in Our World	Gareth Stevens	K–5
Scholastic News Nonfiction Readers. Math	Scholastic	1–2
Math Adventures	Gareth Stevens	2–3
My First Steps to Math	Child's World	K–1
Making Math Easy	Enslow	2–4
Exploring Math	Bridgestone Books	K–1
Magical Math	Wiley	3–6
Math in the Real World	Facts On File	4–6
Concepts	Rourke	K–1
Mighty Math	Children's World	1–3

Figure 4.4 Math Series 1

Journaling: Encourage students to write about the following: Have you ever felt that a math curse was placed on you? When? How did you break the curse? See Figure 4.4 for a list of book series for grades K–6.

Fractals, Googles and Other Mathematical Tales (1993) by Theoni Pappas

(Grades 6–8) This selection, featuring Penrose the cat, introduces a variety of easy-to-follow mathematical ideas and minds-on activities. Students will enjoy the many imaginative explanations of the topics addressed, such as "Watch Out for the Googles" and "Penrose Meets Mr. Abacus."

Suggestions for Classroom Use

1. Ask students to explore how exponents work. Next, ask the students to write the exponential forms for million, billion, trillion, quadrillion, quintillion, sextillion, octillion, nonillion, and decillion. Can they make it to vigintillion?
2. Carl Friedrich Gauss (1777–1855) was a famous mathematician. Ask students to investigate his mathematical discoveries.
3. Ask students to investigate the history of Π.
4. A French mathematician, M. Tremaux, generated a method to solve any maze. Encourage students to investigate this method and try it out with an actual maze.

The Babylonian system is the oldest known place value system. Allow students to research this number system.

Journaling: Encourage students to write about the following: Why was the number 0 developed?

Works Cited

National Council of Teachers of Mathematics. *Principles and Standards for School Mathematics.* Reston, VA: National Council of Teachers of Mathematics, 2000.

Children's Books Cited

Anno, Mitsumasa. *Anno's Magic Seeds*. Illus. Mitsumasa Anno. New York: Penguin Putnam, 1995.

Birch, David. *The King's Chessboard*. Illus. Devis Grebu. New York: Puffin, 1988.

Enzensberger, Hans Magnus. *The Number Devil A Mathematical Adventure*. Illus. Rotraut Susanne Berner. New York: Henry Holt, 1997.

Pappas, Theoni. *The Adventures of Penrose the Mathematical Cat*. San Carlos, CA: Wide World, 1997.

———. *Fractals, Googles and Other Mathematical Tales*. San Carlos, CA: Wide World, 1993.

Scieszka, Jon, and Lane Smith. *Math Curse*. Illus. Lane Smith. New York: Viking, 1995.

Additional Titles

Downey, Tika. *How the Arabs Invented Algebra: The History of the Concept of Variables* (PowerMath). New York: PowerKids, 2004. (Grades 6–8)

> The first part of the book explains that the history of algebra starts with the Wisdom House, a place of learning established by Al-Mamun, the ruler of the Arabic-Islamic Empire in 830 A.D. Next, an important mathematician named Muhammad ben Musa al-Khwarizmi wrote a book that introduced algebra. Other scholars followed, eventually making it possible for ideas about algebra to travel to Europe and other parts of the world. In the second part of the book, readers are asked to take on the persona of a merchant and to use algebra to solve seven problems. The book is written with reluctant, struggling readers in mind and includes a glossary.

Edens, Cooper. *How Many Bears?* Illus. Marjett C. Schille. New York: Simon and Schuster, 1994. (Grades 1–3)

> Little Animal Town is a country town where animals manage all of the stores, from the giraffe-owned Soda Fountain to the Gorgeous Gator Beauty Parlor. The first page welcomes the reader into Little Animal Town and explains that the equations on each page will help the reader come closer to figuring out the number of bears needed to work at the bakery shown on the last page. Readers have to look closely at the watercolor illustrations so that they can count the number of tigers who work at the candy store and rhinos who run the grocery.

Janeczko, Paul B. *Top Secret: A Handbook of Codes, Ciphers, and Secret Writing*. Illus. Jenna LaReau. Cambridge, MA: Candlewick, 2004. (Grade 4–8)

> We use codes all the time, from zip codes to International Standard Book Numbers (ISBN). This guide explains commonly used codes and helps readers create and decipher codes. There are also exercises and tips for creating a code-making kit.

Lichtman, Wendy. *Do the Math: Secrets, Lies, and Algebra* (Do the Math). New York: HarperCollins, 2007. (Grades 5–8)

> Eighth-grader Tess is so good at algebra. She uses it and other mathematics concepts to understand the people around her, even her friends, whom she secretly nicknames s^5 (Sammy) and /M/ (Miranda). She also uses math to rationalize revealing what she knows about a

classmate who stole an exam (additive property of equality), determine how often a peer is dishonest (percentages), and imagine how a family friend died (graphs). Also see the author's *The Writing on the Wall* (2008).

McKibbon, Hugh William. *The Token Gift*. Illus. Scott Cameron. Toronto, Ontario: Annick. (Grades 1–4)

When Rajrishi, or wise one, tells his wife that he wonders what it would have been like if he had been a king, she reminds him of the extraordinary life he has lived and how he invented chess. When King Raju discovers that the man who invented chess lives in his kingdom, he offers Rajrishi a reward. He refuses the gift, pointing out that he is old and wealthy, but the king insists. Rajrishi asks the king to place rice on a large chessboard in the middle of the palace floor. The king thinks the request was simple and promises to place one grain of rice on the first square of the chessboard, two grains on the second, four grains on the third, and so on until the board is full of rice. After consulting the royal mathematician, the king discovers he does not have enough rice to honor Rajrishi's request. Embarrassed, King Raju tells Rajrishi that he is now the king, since King Raju must step down from the throne because he did not keep his word. For a while Rajrishi is happy to be king, but then he becomes disappointed. Later, he returns to Raju and reinstates him as king. This book is similar to *The King's Chessboard,* by David Birch.

Murphy, Stuart J. *Less Than Zero* (Math Start). Illus. Frank Remkiewicz. New York: HarperCollins, 2003. (Grades 1–3)

All of Perry's friends have ice scooters, and he wants one, too. His parents say he can have one if he earns the nine clams needed to purchase it. Perry earns four clams after he trims the ice outside his house. Excited about his earnings, he makes a graph so that he can keep track of his finances. But when Perry goes out to have a good time with his friends, he spends the four clams and borrows a clam from a friend. When Perry looks at his graph, he realizes his clams have dwindled to fewer than zero. Throughout the book, Perry experiences fluctuations in his earnings. An author's note explains that the concept of negative numbers is a tool that will assist students with learning algebraic concepts.

Chapter 5

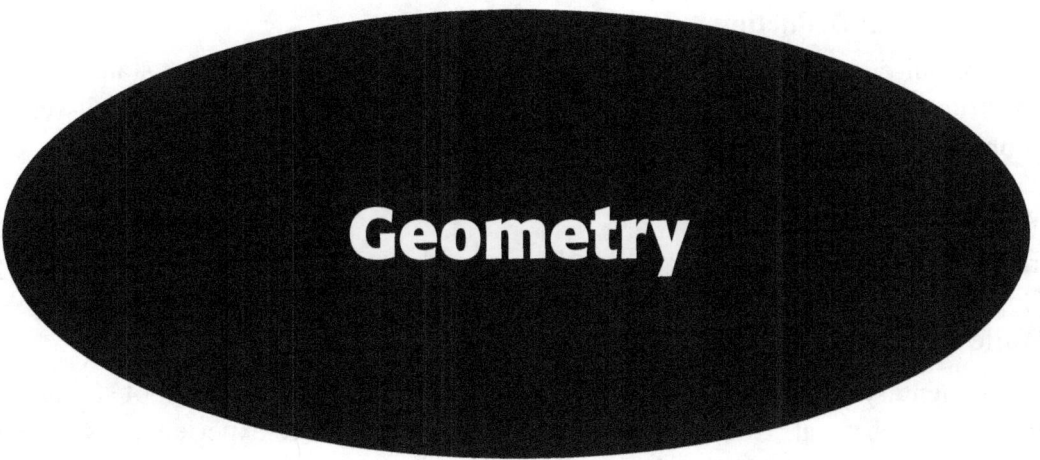

Geometry

Geometry is recognized as a fundamental concept of the mathematics program for elementary and middle school students (NCTM 2000). Moreover, a new appreciation of theoretical perspectives and understandings has influenced its importance in the mathematics curriculum (Van De Walle 399). For example, Dutch educators and researchers Pierre van Hiele and Dina van Hiele-Geldof developed a model for geometric thought; that is, they described how students think differently with regard to their geometric understanding. They introduced a hierarchy consisting of five levels that outline how students think and what they think about (Van De Walle 400). It's critical that teachers and librarians be mindful of these levels so that they can provide the necessary geometric learning experiences that not only address current levels of understanding but also challenge students to reach toward the next level.

Level 0: Visualization

Students at this level view shapes on the basis of visual characteristics and how they resemble other objects. Therefore, experiences should focus on drawing and constructing shapes. Students can also begin rudimentary classification systems (Cathcart, Pothier, Vance, and Bezuk 288; Van De Walle 401).

Level 1: Analysis

At this level, students begin thinking in terms of properties. They can identify the properties of different shapes, but they cannot see the relationships among these properties. Students should be provided with experiences that concentrate specifically on the properties of geometric shapes (Cathcart et al., 288; Van De Walle 402).

Level 2: Informal Deduction

Students are now able to think about and understand the relationship among the properties. They can participate in "if-then" reasoning and informal deductive arguments (Cathcart et al., 288; Van De Walle 403).

Level 3: Formal Deduction

At the formal-deduction level, students can begin working with abstract statements and constructing formal proofs. This level of understanding is needed for a high-school geometry class (Cathcart et al., 289; Van De Walle 403–404).

Level 4: Rigor

Here, students are able to work with abstract mathematical ideas and axiomatic systems. College mathematics students are generally at this level (Cathcart et al., 289; Van De Walle 404).

Most elementary children are at Levels 0 and 1, while some middle school students reach Level 2 (Cathcart et al., 289). Therefore, providing appropriate experiences is necessary to address the student's level of understanding.

Geometry Expectations

Geometry expectations for elementary and middle school students, as articulated by the National Council of Teachers of Mathematics, include the ability to recognize, draw, and compare two- and three-dimensional shapes; describe their attributes and parts; describe, name, and interpret relative positions, directions, and distance; and find and name locations. Students should recognize and apply flips, slides, turns, and symmetry. Students should also be able to use visualization and spatial reasoning, geometric reasoning, and problem solving (NCTM 96, 164, 232). A complete listing of the geometry standard expectations can be found in the *Principles and Standards for School Mathematics* (NCTM 96, 164, 232).

Using Mathematics Literature
Sir Cumference and the First Round Table (1997) by Cindy Neuschwander

(Grades 3–6) The author does an excellent job of introducing mathematical geometric terminology through the use of characters. Sir Cumference is a knight in the land of Camelot and is married to Lady Di of the town of Ameter. Together, they have a son named Radius. King Arthur, the ruler of Camelot, calls all the knights of the land together to devise a plan in case war is proclaimed by their neighbors, the Circumscribers. Sir Cumference is charged with designing a table where all the knights can sit comfortably during their discussions. Through trial and error, Sir Cumference presents different models for the table, only to find that a round table works best. Neuschwander has written other Sir Cumference books, including *Sir Cumference and the Dragon of Pi, Sir Cumference and the Great Knight of Angleland, Sir Cumference and the Sword in the Cone,* and *Sir Cumference and the Isle of Immeter.* This series is a must for any library.

Suggestions for Classroom Use

1. A teacher resource book, *Round Table Geometry,* provides fun learning activities that complement *Sir Cumference and the First Round Table.* Offered for $9.95, the book can be ordered at <www.charlesbridge.com>.

2. Provide the students with several circular shapes, or pre-cut circles. Show them how to use string and a ruler to determine the circle's radius, diameter, and circumference.

3. Provide students with two pre-cut rectangles (20 feet by 5 feet). Ask the students to cut a square, parallelogram, triangle, octagon, and oval out of the large rectangles. Students will enjoy recreating the different tables that Sir Cumference introduced.

4. The National Council of Teachers of Mathematics' Illuminations Web site <http://illuminations.nctm.org/ActivityDetail.aspx?id = 116> offers a "Circle Tool" activity that students in grades 3–8 can use to compare the circumference and area of a circle to its radius and diameter. This interactive applet allows students to investigate their relationships.

Journaling: Ask students to investigate life in the Middle Ages, including such topics as knighthood, castles, and jousts and tournaments.

Grandfather Tang's Story (1990) by Ann Tompert

(Grades 1–6) *Grandfather Tang's Story* is a delightful tale that introduces tangrams to students. Grandfather Tang and his granddaughter, Little Soo, enjoy a story about the fox fairies, Chou and Wu Ling. According to Chinese folklore, fox fairies are believed to have supernatural transformation powers. Throughout the story, they both challenge each other to quickly change into different kinds of animals until they become too distracted to see that they are in danger of being killed by a hunter. Grandfather Tang illustrates these animals with a set of tangrams. A traceable tangram is provided in the resource material in the back of the book.

Suggestions for Classroom Use

1. Tangrams are Chinese puzzles that stimulate special abilities. They are made up of seven geometric shapes (each piece is called a tan), and, when assembled correctly, they make a square. Tangrams can also be used to create different pictures. The National Library of Virtual Manipulatives <http://www.nlvm.usu.edu> has a geometry content strand that provides virtual tangrams that students can explore and use to improve their spatial abilities by trying to re-create the different pictures provided with tangrams.

2. When working with tangram puzzles, students will need to practice with flips, turns, and slides. You can provide students with different geometric images made from the tangrams and require them to re-create a mirror image. The original geometric image must be different on at least one side, requiring a different mirror image. Motivation levels will remain high while students gain experience with flipping, sliding, and turning the tangram pieces.

3. Tangrams can be used to create thousands of images! Provide the students with a list of objects, animals, and so on, and require them to create the images with tangrams. The Internet offers numerous resources of pictures for the students to recreate.
Allow students to create their own tangram set.

✦ Using a sheet of 8.5 × 11 inch paper, fold the short side so that it lies along the long side, and open it.

✦ Fold the other short side of the bottom of the paper up to the bottom of the newly formed triangle, and open it. Cut off the rectangle you just folded.

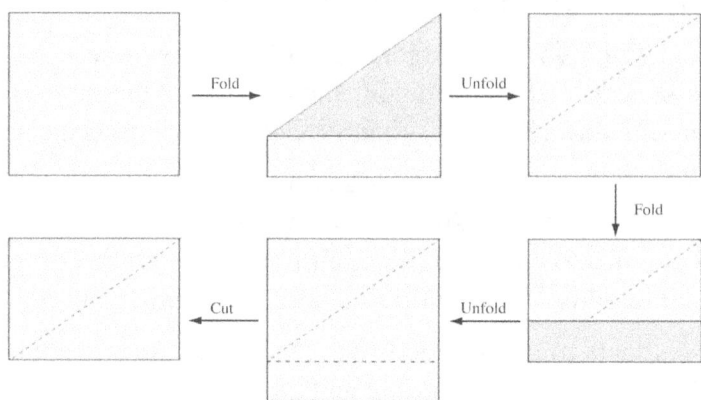

✦ Cut the square along the diagonal you created when folding.

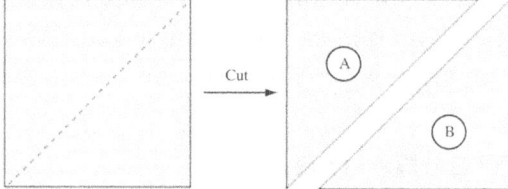

✦ Fold one of the triangles you created in half, and cut the triangle along the fold to create two smaller triangles.

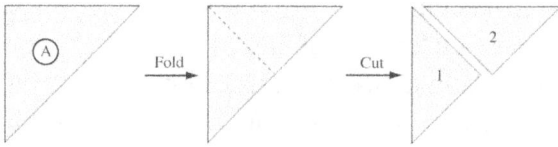

✦ Using the other triangle created, mark the center of the hypotenuse. Fold the corner of the right angle to the center mark on the hypotenuse. Cut on the fold.

64 *Mathematics in the K–8 Classroom and Library*

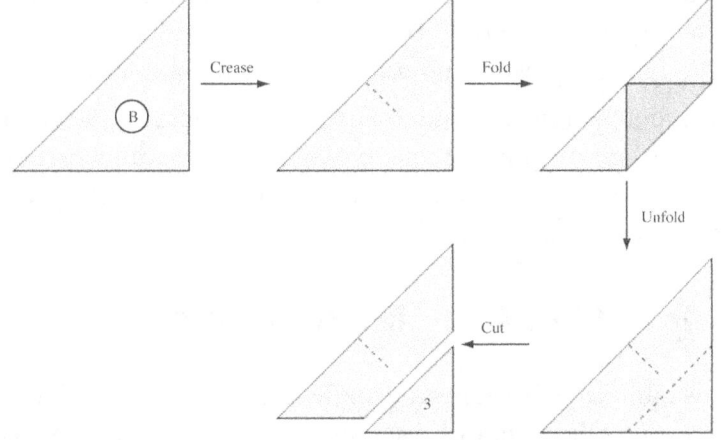

✦ Using the trapezoid piece, fold it in half, and then fold it again. Cut along both folds.

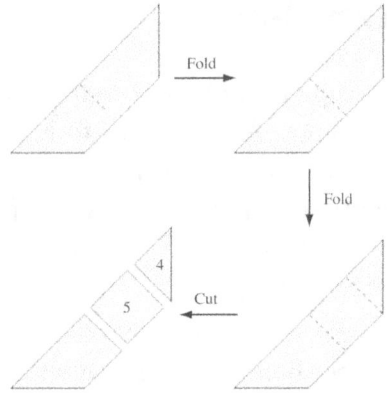

✦ Using the remaining small trapezoid, fold, and cut it into two. Fold the obtuse angle to the right angle, and cut. These are the sixth and seventh pieces of your tangram puzzle.

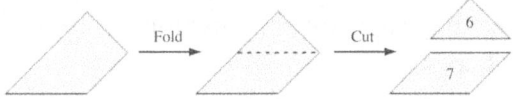

4. You can also make a set of tangrams using a 4 × 4 inch square, cutting along the highlighted dimensions. A template for tangrams is also provided in the Appendix.

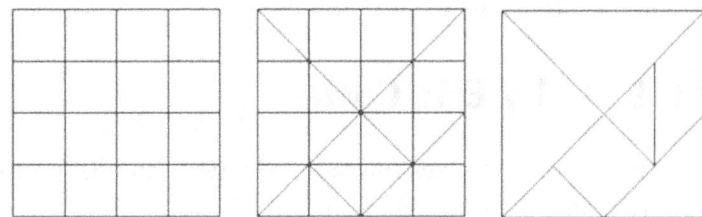

Chapter 5: Geometry 65

5. Tangrams can also be used to promote problem solving. For example, ask the students if they can create a square using only two pieces, three pieces, four pieces, and so on. You can do the same type of questioning with creating rectangles and other shapes.

Journaling: Ask students to investigate the history of tangrams. There are many Chinese folktales that explain their origin; one tale explains that tangrams originated from a pane of broken glass intended for use in an ancient royal palace. Students may also enjoy devising their own tale of the tangrams' origin.

The Greedy Triangle (1994) by Marilyn Burns

(Grades K–6) This humorous book is an excellent introduction to shapes. A triangle has a wonderful life as a slice of pie, half of a sandwich, and so on, but one day it gets greedy and wants to change into another shape. The triangle goes to the shapeshifter, who changes it into a quadrilateral, a pentagon, a hexagon, and then back to a triangle. Descriptions of where the different shapes are found in everyday life are provided.

Suggestions for Classroom Use

1. Provide students with a set of pattern blocks. Pattern blocks are color-coded manipulatives that come in six geometric shapes. Ask students to identify the different properties of each shape and to generate a definition of each shape on their list. Students will enjoy identifying different shapes not mentioned in the literature selection (e.g., rhombus, cone, circle) and stating where they are found in their environment. Hold a competition to see which student can develop the longest list!

2. Ask students to create different shapes on geoboards. Geoboards are plastic boards with pegs placed in an array. Rubber bands can be stretched around the pegs to create different shapes, patterns, and designs. The teacher or librarian can hold up a drawing of a shape and ask the students to represent it on their geoboards. Especially appealing, geoboards allow students to explore different shapes in a hands-on manner.

3. Provide students with a set of attribute blocks. Attribute blocks are manipulatives that have four different features: shape, color, size, and thickness. They also come in four different shapes: circles, hexagons, squares, and triangles. Students need experiences with sorting and classifying shapes. They can develop some type of sorting scheme based on the properties of the shapes.

4. Students can play "What's My Shape?" The teacher or librarian can describe the different properties of different shapes while the students guess which shape is being described. This activity promotes precise geometric vocabulary.

Journaling: Ask the students to explore the names of different-sided shapes and to rename three of the shapes. Don't forget to ask them to explain why they think the new name is appropriate. See Figure 5.1 for a list of polygon names.

Draw Me a Star (1994) by Eric Carle

(Grades K–2) This simple story focuses on an artist who uses different geometric shapes to draw a star, a sun, a tree, and, eventually, a universe.

Name	Number of Sides	Name	Number of Sides
Henagon (or monogon)	1	Hendecagon	11
Digon	2	Dodecagon	12
Triangle (or trigon)	3	Tridecagon (or triskaidecagon)	13
Quadrilateral (or tetragon)	4	Tetradecagon (or tetrakaidecagon)	14
Pentagon	5	Pentadecagon (or quindecagon, or pentakaidecagon)	15
Hexagon	6	Hexadecagon (or hexakaidecagon)	16
Heptagon	7	Heptadecagon (or heptakaidecagon)	17
Octagon	8	Octadecagon (or octakaidecagon)	18
Enneagon (or nonagon)	9	Enneadecagon (or enneakaidecagon, or nonadecagon)	19
Decagon	10	Icosagon	20

Figure 5.1 Polygon Names

Suggestions for Classroom Use

1. The drawing of the star provides a wonderful opportunity to explore the different types of angles (i.e., right, acute, and obtuse) and the different types of triangles (i.e., right, equilateral, isosceles, scalene, obtuse). Students can create the different angles and triangles on geoboards.

2. Origami is the Japanese art of paper folding. Using only geometric folding and crease patterns, objects and designs are created. There are numerous Web sites on the Internet that show how to design stars using origami. A few include:

   <www.origami-resource-center.com/stars.html>

   <www.dltk-kids.com/WORLD//JAPAN/morigamistar.htm>

   <www.geocities.com/mukhopadhyay/creation/star/html>

3. Students need numerous opportunities to explore the different geometric shapes. Designing stars with pattern blocks and attribute blocks allows students to experience what it is like to create different shapes.

4. Eric Carle used colored tissue paper and paint to create the illustrations in *Draw Me a Star*. He produced textures in his illustrations by painting on the tissue paper with different artist's brushes. Carle tore the tissue paper to make the different shapes needed for the illustrations and glued them onto an illustration board. Students can create their own illustrations of geometric shapes using a similar technique.

5. Students can try to re-create all the pictures drawn in the story with tangrams!

Journaling: Researching the different names of stars and constellations will keep students' motivation at high levels. Proper names, Greek letter names, catalogue numbers, and variable stars are areas that can be investigated.

Mummy Math: An Adventure in Geometry (2005) by Cindy Neuschwander

(Grades 3–6) Twins Matt and Bibi travel to Egypt with their parents, famous scientists who have been invited to search for the mummy of an ancient pharaoh. Once in Egypt, Matt, Bibi, and their dog, Riley, get locked in a pyramid and decide to search for the mummy themselves. While searching, they discover a mysterious message based on geometric solids. The author introduces eight geometric solids (e.g., sphere, tetrahedron, rectangular prism) through various clues the twins use to find the ancient mummy.

Suggestions for Classroom Use

1. *Mummy Math* introduces eight geometric solids: cone, cylinder, cube, sphere, pyramid, tetrahedron, rectangular prism, and triangular prism. Provide the students with a concrete example of each of these shapes. (Solid manipulatives or real-world examples such as soup cans or shoe boxes can be used.) Have the students generate some sort of classification system based on the characteristics of these shapes.

2. Provide students with copies of different geometric nets. A geometric net is a two-dimensional figure that can be folded into a geometric solid. Ask the students to predict the shapes the nets can be folded into. This is a wonderful opportunity for students to see what geometric terminology, such as edge, face, vertices, parallel, base, and elements, actually looks like. Templates for different geometric nets are provided in the Appendix. Students can cut out the shapes, fold them along the lines, and then fold over and glue the shaded parts to create different geometric solids.

3. Give students different shapes, and ask them to develop geometric nets according to the shapes. Next, students can actually test their nets to see if they can fold into the actual shapes. This activity requires higher-level thinking skills.

4. This is a wonderful opportunity to connect mathematics and science! Have your students create an actual prism! Detailed directions are offered on the Internet at <http://www.eosweb.larc.nasa.gov/EDDOCS/RadiationBudget/prism.html> <http://www.sciencetoymaker.org/prism/assembl.html>

5. Working with solids provides a direct connection to working with volume. Ask students to compare the volume of different shapes. They can actually test different shapes (sand or other granular substance) to determine which has the greatest or least volume.

Journaling: Students will enjoy exploring the ancient Egyptian number system and the mathematical wonders of the Great Pyramid of Khufu from the Fourth Dynasty. They will be amazed at many of the interesting mathematical wonders. Ask them to jot down ideas that interest them. See Figure 5.2 for a list of math literature authors and Figure 5.3 for a list of math series books.

Librarians and teachers turn to the following authors repeatedly for children's literature that supports NCTM content standards:

David M. Adler

Mitsumasa Anno

Marilyn Burns

Dayle Ann Dodds

Lois Ehlert

Tana Hoban

Loreen Leedy

Barbara McGrath

Bruce McMillan

Stuart J. Murphy

Cindy Neuschwander

Jerry Pallotta

Elinor Pinczes

David M. Schwartz

Greg Tang

Robert Wells

Figure 5.2 Math Literature Authors

Series Title	Publisher	Grade Level
Know Your Shapes	Picture Window	K–2
Math Monsters	Weekly Reader	K–2
Sandcastle	Abdo	K–2
Marilyn Burns Brainy Day Books	Scholastic	K–3
A Math Adventure Series	Charlesbridge	2–6
Hello Reader, Math	Scholastic	K–6
Math Success	Enslow	5–8
Math Alive!	Marshall Cavendish	5–8
PowerMath	PowerKids	5–8

Figure 5.3 Math Series 2

Works Cited

Cathcart, W. George, Yvonne Pothier, James Vance, and Nadine Bezuk. *Learning Mathematics in Elementary and Middle Schools.* Upper Saddle River, NJ: Pearson, 2006.

National Council of Teachers of Mathematics. *Principles and Standards for School Mathematics.* Reston, VA: National Council of Teachers of Mathematics, 2000.

Van De Walle, John, Karen Karp, and Jennifer Bay-Williams. *Elementary and Middle School Mathematics.* Boston: Allyn and Bacon, 2010.

Children's Books Cited

Burns, Marilyn. *The Greedy Triangle.* Illus. Gordon Silveria. New York: Scholastic, 1994.

Carle, Eric. *Draw Me a Star.* New York: Penguin Putnam, 1992.

Neuschwander, Cindy. *Mummy Math: An Adventure in Geometry.* Illus. Bryan Lango. New York: Henry Holt, 2005.

———. *Sir Cumference and the Dragon of Pi.* Illus. Wayne Geehan. Watertown, MA: Charlesbridge, 2004.

———. *Sir Cumference and the First Round Table.* Illus. Wayne Geehan. Watertown, MA: Charlesbridge, 1997.

———. *Sir Cumference and the Great Night of Angleland.* Illus. Wayne Geehan. Watertown, MA: Charlesbridge, 2001.

———. *Sir Cumference and the Isle of Immeter.* Illus. Wayne Geehan. Watertown, MA: Charlesbridge, 2006.

———. *Sir Cumference and the Sword in the Cone.* Illus. Wayne Geehan. Watertown, MA: Charlesbridge, 2003.

Tompert, Ann. *Grandfather Tang's Story.* Illus. Robert Andrew Parker. New York: Crown, 1990.

Additional Titles

Adler, David. *Shape Up!: Fun with Triangles and Other Polygons.* Illus. Nancy Tobin. New York: Holiday House, 1998. (Grades 2–5)

> Food (pretzels, cheese, and bread) is used to introduce different types of triangles, lines, and quadrilaterals. Readers are encouraged to use graph paper to draw a quadrilateral, hexagon, trapezoid, and so on. Speech bubbles and cartoonish illustrations establish a fun tone throughout the book. A list of the characteristics (sides and degrees) of all of the shapes and angles discussed in the book is provided.

Dodds, Dayle Ann. *The Shape of Things.* Illus. Julie Lacome. New York: Candlewick. (Grades K–1)

> Colorful cut-paper collages introduce squares, triangles, rectangles, diamonds, ovals, and more. The illustrations make it clear that shapes make up familiar objects like windows, kites, eggs, and so on.

Ellis, Julie. *What's Your Angle, Pythagoras?: A Math Adventure.* Illus. Phyllis Hornung. Watertown, MA: Charlesbridge, 2004. (Grades 3–5)

This fictionalized story about Pythagoras's childhood begins with a curious, busy boy. While traveling with his father from their home in Samos to Alexandria, the boy meets Neferheperhersekeper, a builder who shows him how he uses a rope to make right angles. Pythagoras studies the idea and eventually develops the Pythagorean Theorem.

Friedman, Aileen. *A Cloak for the Dreamer* (A Marilyn Burns Brainy Day Book). Illus. Kim Howard. New York: Scholastic, 1994. (Grades K–3)

A tailor decides to determine his three sons' talents by asking each one to make a colorful cloak for the Archduke. Ivan and Alex want to become tailors, so they dutifully cut and arrange shapes into cloaks that will please their father and the Archduke. Influenced by his desire to travel the world, Misha uses pieces of fabric he has cut into circles to design a cloak. The tailor likes Ivan and Alex's cloaks so much that he invites them to work alongside him as tailors. Although he praises Misha's effort, he tells Misha he knows that he does not want to be a tailor. The tailor, Ivan, and Alex improve Misha's cloak and give it to him as a goodbye gift. An author's note explains how the shapes Ivan and Alex use are able to fit together to form a cloak while the circles Misha uses cannot.

Greene, Rhonda Gowler. *When a Line Bends . . . A Shape Begins*. Illus. James Kaczman. New York: Houghton Mifflin, 1997. (Grades K–2)

Rhyming text explains that all shapes begin with a line. Each double-page spread bleeds and is filled with watercolor and ink illustrations that offer examples of lines, circles, squares, triangles, diamonds, rectangles, ovals, and so on, in a child's world.

Hayhurst, Chris. *Euclid: The Great Geometer* (The Library of Greek Philosophers). New York: Rosen, 2006. (Grades 6–8)

Though little is known about Euclid's personal life, he is well known as one of the first to write a book about geometry. While he founded his own school and is believed to have taught Archimedes, a great geometer, he was also a distinguished math teacher at the Museum in Egypt. A detailed chapter explains the significance of Euclid's *The Elements*. Descriptions of ancient Greece, the origins of mathematics, and the lives of scholars, including Thales, Pythagoras, and Eudoxus, are included.

Hoban, Tana. *Cubes, Cones, Cylinders and Spheres*. New York: Greenwillow, 2000. (Grades K–5)

Photographs indicate that cubes, cones, cylinders, and spheres can be found all around us. A girl carries two ice cream cones, a boy blows bubbles, a boy carries wrapped gifts, and a beautiful castle sits amid lush hedges. Some of the bordered photographs—the one with the teddy bears wearing hats and the photo of a child's hand using sugar cubes to build a castle—show more than one shape.

———. *So Many Circles, So Many Squares*. New York: Greenwillow, 1998. (Grades K–2)

Full-color photographs show wheels, tomatoes, onions, dartboards, and boxes to help reinforce the idea that shapes are all around us.

Jones, Christianne C. *Two Short, Two Long: A Book about Rectangles* (Know Your Shapes). Minneapolis, MN: Picture Window, 2006. (Grade K–2)

A little boy—with a brown head shaped like a rectangle—writes a report about rectangles. The rhyming text emphasizes the rectangular objects the boy sees each day: school bus, locker, desk, window, and so on. Activities and references are appended. Other books by Jones include *Four Sides the Same: A Book about Squares* (2006) and *Party of Three: A Book about Triangles* (2006).

Kassirer, Sue. *Math Fair Blues* (Math Matters). Illus. Jerry Smath. New York: Kane, 2001. (Grade 1–2)

Seth's teacher wants him to work on his math project, but all he can do is think about practicing with his band. Mr. Wall tells Seth that his band is welcome to perform at the math fair, but the members still have to submit a project. Seth and the band are so busy practicing and making costumes filled with geometric shapes that they forget to do a math project. Their performance receives a round of applause, and their principal assumes that their costumes are their project and gives them the Most Artistic Math Project award. The book ends with a 2-D shapes chart.

Lasky, Kathryn. *The Librarian Who Measured the Earth*. Illus. Kevin Hawkes. Boston: Little, Brown, 1994. (Grades 3–5)

This book introduces Eratosthenes, the chief librarian in Alexandria, Egypt, who solved geometry problems and wrote literature before studying mathematical information about the Earth. Using the mathematics established before him (i.e., ratio tables, formulas for measuring the circumference of a circle, and knowledge about angles and lines), he developed a formula for calculating the earth's circumference. An author's note explains that little information exists about the Greek scholar. A bibliography of sources used by the author and the illustrator is included.

MacDonald, Suse. *Sea Shapes*. San Diego, CA: Harcourt Brace, 1994. (Grade K)

One shape is the focus of each double-page spread. On the left-hand page, the name of the shape is above three or four images that show the shape and how the shape is a significant part of an animal's body. For example, on the page marked semicircle, the first image shows a semicircle, the next shows two jellyfish with short tentacles, and the last one shows two fully developed jellyfish. The right-hand page shows the sea creature swimming around with other creatures. Star, circle, square, heart, triangle, diamond, rectangle, and hexagon are among the included shapes. The book ends with a "Sea Facts" section that gives information about each animal featured.

McGrath, Barbara Barbieri. *The M&M's Color Pattern Book*. Illus. Roger Glass. Watertown, MA: Charlesbridge, 2002. (Grades K–2)

M&M's are used to teach sorting and patterns.

Metropolitan Museum of Art. *Museum Shapes*. New York: Little, Brown, 2005. (Grades K–3)

Shapes and famous works of art found at the Metropolitan Museum of Art are introduced in this colorful book. One page (filled with hints) prompts the reader to identify a shape seen in the picture on the opposite page, while the following page offers four opportunities to see squares found in four different works of art. A final page shows the shape alone in the middle of the page. Familiar shapes like squares, triangles, and rectangles are included alongside possibly less familiar shapes like arch and crescent. The last few pages of the book show the pictures and include captions for each piece of art that list the artist, the medium, and the artwork's actual dimensions.

Micklethwait, Lucy. *I Spy Shapes in Art*. New York: Greenwillow, 2004. (Grades K–2)

A foreword offers adults tips that make learning about art and shapes interesting to young readers. The author uses the "I Spy" game to encourage readers to identify shapes (e.g., oval, diamond, cone, and sphere) found in classic paintings. Works by artists such as Georgia O'Keeffe, Henri Matisse, Paul Klee, Andy Warhol, and Auguste Herbin are included. An "I Spy" phrase is printed in large font on the left-hand pages with the artist's name and the title of the painting underneath. The book ends with a list of featured shapes and information about the paintings.

Moranville, Sharelle Byars. *A Higher Geometry*. New York: Henry Holt, 2006. (Grade 8)

Math concepts come so easily to 15-year-old Anna that she wants to enter a math competition and study math in college. Since women rarely pursued math-related careers in the 1950s, Anna's family and friends do not understand her ambitions. Surprisingly, her relationship with Mike gives her the courage and support she needs to stay true to her talents.

Onyefulu, Ifeoma. *A Triangle for Adaora: An African Book of Shapes*. New York: Dutton Children's Books, 2000. (Grades K–2)

The narrator is worried because his cousin Adaora refuses to eat paw-paw because she does not want to ruin the star shape in the center of the fruit. The narrator tells Adaora he will help her find her favorite shape, a triangle, if she starts eating paw-paw again. They look all around and find many shapes—square, rectangle, oval, diamond—before finally finding a triangle. By the end of the story, there is another problem: Adaora will not stop wearing the dress filled with shapes that Aunt Felicia made.

Pallotta, Jerry. *Twizzlers: Shapes and Patterns*. Illus. Rob Bolster. New York: Scholastic, 2002. (Grades K–3)

When an architect visits the class and teaches about shapes, one child uses her Twizzlers to create shapes and patterns.

Pearsall, Shelley. *All of the Above: A Novel*. Illus. Javaka Steptoe. New York: Little, Brown, 2006. (Grade 5–8)

Multiple narrators tell the story of what happens when a group of students and a teacher decide they will form a math club and build a tetrahedron so big it will earn them fame. Each student describes personal problems and how they all find comfort in the math club, while Mr. Collins's sections give facts about tetrahedrons. When club's first effort to build a tetrahedron is thwarted, they, along with members of the community, rededicate themselves to the project. This story was influenced by students in a Cleveland, Ohio, middle school who built a tetrahedron in 2002.

Rau, Dana Meachen. *A Star in My Orange: Looking for Nature's Shapes* (Fun Early Math). Brookfield, CT: Millbrook Press, 2002. (Grades K–2)

Beginning with stars in the sky, the author emphasizes the abundance of shapes and patterns found in nature (e.g., snowflakes, daisies, pinecones, seahorses).

Reisberg, Joanne A. *Zachary Zormer Shape Transformer: A Math Adventure*. Illus. David Hohn. Watertown, MA: Charlesbridge, 2006. (Grades 2–4)

Zachary Zormer's favorite day of the week was Friday until his teacher encourages the students to bring in something to measure, giving them opportunities to determine the area, perimeter, length, and width of objects. Zachary forgets to bring something, but he manages to use a piece of paper in his pocket to meet the requirement. All of his classmates enjoy his presentation except Tyler. The next week, Tyler hides the rectangular object Zachary plans to share, but it does not matter. A quick thinker, Zachary once again uses his resources. This time he tells the class the measurements of a piece of paper and shows them how to create a "big, zigzagging frame." The illustrations are colorful and detailed. The chalkboard lists the assignments for Friday's lessons on measurement clearly. For example, one Friday, the note on the board announces: "Bring in a rectangle and tell us how you found its perimeter." Detailed instructions in the back of the book tell readers how to create Zachary's transformations.

Roza, Greg. *Where We Play Sports: Measuring the Perimeters of Polygons* (Power Math). New York: PowerKids, 2004. (Grades 3–5)

After defining "polygon" and "perimeter," the book describes the courts, fields, and other areas where the most popular sports are played: basketball, football, baseball, soccer, tennis, and lacrosse. A color photograph of the field indicates the length and width of the field, and readers are shown how to add to discover the perimeter.

Smith, Albert G. *Cut and Assemble 3-D Geometric Shapes: Ten Models in Full Color*. Mineola, NY: Dover, 1986. (Grades 2–6)

The instructions and diagrams for making 10 geometric shapes, including tetrahedrons, octahedrons, cubes, trapezohedrons, and icosahedrons, are featured.

Swinburne, Stephen R. *Lots and Lots of Zebra Stripes: Patterns in Nature*. Honesdale, PA: Boyds Mill, 1998. (Grades K–2)

Before the photoessay begins, a foreword explains that patterns can be found in nature, food, and in homes. The photos show patterns in flowers, pumpkins, spider webs, trees, strawberries, tiles, and so on. The text on the final pages of the book asks readers to look for patterns in several pictures.

CHAPTER 6

The National Council of Teachers of Mathematics recognizes measurement as one of the most extensively used mathematical applications and maintains that efforts should be made to help students understand and apply the concept of measurement to their everyday lives (NCTM 103). Although measurement is widely used and connects to all content areas, students experience difficulty with many of the expectations of measurement, such as using a ruler and understanding the foundations of measurement formulas, including those used for calculating perimeter, area, surface area, and volume (Cathcart, Pothier, Vance, and Bezuk, 321; Van De Walle 396). Concentrated efforts need to be made by the teacher and the librarian to provide students with a conceptual understanding of the meaning of measurement (e.g., what it means to find the perimeter or surface area) before any abstract mathematical formula is introduced. Additionally, these efforts should be authentic and student-centered. If students are provided with rich and genuine experiences, they will gain an understanding of measurable attributes and will be able to apply the appropriate measurement methods and tools.

What activities or experiences qualify as "rich and genuine"? A student-centered, rich, and genuine experience is one that allows students to actually use measuring tools and apply measurement concepts to realistic situations. See Figure 6.1 for a list of math series books related to measurement.

Measurement Expectations

It is important for the librarian to have some understanding of the expectations for measurement, as identified by national and state standards. This understanding will allow the librarian and teacher to work collaboratively in selecting literature books that specifically

Series Title	Publisher	Grade Level
The Calendar	Capstone	K–3
How Do We Measure?	Blackbirch/ThomsonGale	3–6
Let's Measure	Abdo	K–3
Measure Up!	Marshall Cavendish	4–7
First Facts. Learning about Money.	Capstone	K–2

Figure 6.1 Math Series (Measurement)

focus on the concepts under study, as well as assisting them in generating instructional strategies to complement the story.

According to the NCTM Measurement Standards and Expectations, students, grades PK–12, should understand measurement systems and processes such as the attributes of weight, area, length, volume, time, and money. They should also be able to apply measurement tools and formulas to determine accurate measures. Specific expectations are offered by the NCTM according to grade bands (PK–2, 3–5, 6–8, 9–12) in *Principles and Standards for School Mathematics* (102, 170, 240).

Using Mathematics Literature
Twelve Snails to One Lizard: A Tale of Mischief and Measurement (1997) by Susan Hightower

(Grades K–1) Milo Beaver is determined to save the pond before the end of the rainy season. If a dam is not built, all the rain water will flow downstream, leaving the beavers' pond dry all summer. Bubba Bullfrog offers his help with building the dam by presenting Milo Beaver with different nonstandard units of measure so that he can precisely cut a branch for the dam. Snails, iguana lizards, and snakes are used to represent inches, feet, and yards to assist Milo Beaver with building the dam.

Suggestions for Classroom Use

1. To provide students with experiences in using nonstandard units of measure, have them identify other nonstandard units of measure to represent inches, feet, and yards. This may include classroom items (e.g., books, a piece of chalk), objects outside the classroom (e.g., insects, worms, leaves), or body parts (fingers, arms). Students can convert these nonstandard units to generate their own measurement system (e.g., 10 beetles = 12 inches).

2. Visit the National Library of Virtual Manipulatives Web site <http://nlvm.usu.edu/en/nav/vLibrary.html>. The measurement site offers activities (e.g., Ladybug Maze and Ladybug Leaf) that require students to visually estimate length.

3. Provide objects that students can compare on the basis of a measurable attribute. For example, students should compare the length of these objects, emphasizing approximate language (e.g., longer, shorter, or about the same).

4. Ask students to build a structure using only nonstandard units of measure. The teacher or librarian can provide the dimensions of the structure in nonstandard form and require the students to convert the nonstandard units into standard units to complete the structure. Students can use popsicle sticks, clay, or paper to build their structure (e.g., house, box).

5. Once the students are comfortable with using nonstandard units of measure, introduce a measuring instrument (ruler). Ask students to measure objects in the classroom. This activity can be altered by providing specific measurements of objects around the classroom and requiring students to find those objects. For example, you might list the following measurements on the board: one foot, eight inches, four feet. First, ask students to look about the room for objects that appear to be one foot long. Once they choose an object, they must measure it to see if it is actually one foot long. If it is not, they have to keep looking until they find an object that is. Students follow this procedure until they have located objects in the room that are equal to each of the measurements on the board.

Journaling: Encourage students to write about the following topic: Pretend that you have washed ashore on a deserted island and must build a raft to take you back to your homeland. Provide a description of the measurements you will use to make the raft, using only nonstandard units of measure made up of items that can be found on the island.

How Tall, How Short, How Faraway (1999) by David A. Adler

(Grades 2–4) This selection can engage children in many problem-solving activities. The story begins by providing the reader with an overview of the measurement system used in ancient Egypt. It proceeds by urging students to measure their own bodies using the ancient Egyptian system. The measuring system of ancient Rome is then introduced, and, again, students are asked to apply this system of measurement. The book ends by introducing the metric system of measurement. Because this selection provides many problem-solving situations for the students, it is an excellent selection for hands-on measurement.

Suggestions for Classroom Use

1. Have the students complete the measurement activities in the selection: measuring their body using the measurement system of ancient Egypt, measuring the length of their neighborhood block using the measurement system of ancient Rome, and measuring items using the customary and metric systems.

2. Provide your students with pictures of several different items (crayons, paper, refrigerator, and so on) and their customary measurements. Ask students to identify which metric measure should also be used to measure that item.

3. Ask students to identify nonstandard units of measure for the metric system. For example, one meter might equal the length of seven chalkboard erasers.

4. Encourage students to investigate the measurement systems of ancient times (e.g., the Mayans of Central America) and compare the systems with today's measurement systems.

5. Ask students to create a "Human Giant" by taking their body measurements and multiplying them by three, four, or five.

Journaling: Encourage students to write about the following: A French priest, Father Gabriel Mouton, proposed the metric system more than 300 years ago. It is based on the distance from the North Pole to the equator (Adler 18). Develop your own measurement system. This includes identifying your point of reference for calculating inches, feet, yards, and miles.

Clocks and More Clocks (1970) by Pat Hutchins

(Grades K–1) Although this is an older book, the selection does a wonderful job of demonstrating time duration. Mr. Higgins finds a clock in the attic, and, to check the accuracy of its time, he buys another clock, which he places in his bedroom. Mr. Higgins then checks the time on both clocks to make sure they are correct. However, each time he checks the different clocks, they show a different time. Since they are displaying different times, he calls the clockmaker to check his clocks. (Mr. Higgins is not taking into account the time it takes to go from his bedroom to the attic.) Using his pocket watch, the clockmaker then shows Mr. Higgins that both times are correct.

Suggestions for Classroom Use

1. To assist students in understanding time duration (e.g., one-half minute and one minute) and in developing a conscious reference point of how long these time units actually are, provide different experiences for the students that represent different times. For example, students can time themselves washing their hands, writing their name, and so on.

    Have the students keep a record of their activities for one day (beginning and ending times). For example,

    7:00 A.M.–7:15 A.M.: Washed up for school.

    7:30 A.M.–7: 46 A.M.: Got dressed for school.

    7:46 A.M.–7:53 A.M.: Brushed hair.

    Once the students complete their daily record of activities, have them figure out the elapsed time for each event.

2. Visit the National Library of Virtual Manipulatives Web site <http://nlvm.usu.edu/en/nav/vLibrary.html>. The measurement site offers activities that require students to match times on digital and analog clocks and to identify elapsed times.

    Students can use *TV Guide* magazine to identify which TV shows they watch during a 24-hour period.

3. The teacher or librarian can develop her own version of a "Beat the Clock" game. For example, two students can compete to determine who can finish a task within a certain amount of time. This can be modified to include other timed games.

4. Visit the ETA/Cuisenaire Web site <http://www.etacuisenaire.com>. This site offers many manipulatives that can be used for teaching time. Some suggested manipulatives include an Elapsed Time Clock, a Time Activity Mat, and a Big Time Learning Clock.

5. Students can also figure out the times of different places around the world when given an initial place and time. The Web site <http://www.timeanddate.com> offers a world clock and time zones, as well as a time zone converter.

How Many? A Dictionary of Units of Measurement
<http://www.unc.edu/~rowlett/units/>

Division of Measurement Standards: Kid's Corner
<http://www.cdfa.ca.gov/dms/kidspage/History.htm>

The Official U.S. Time
<http://www.time.gov/>

U.S. Navy Time Service Department
<http://tycho.usno.navy.mil/what.html>

The World of Measurement
<http://oncampus.richmond.edu/academics/education/projects/webunits/measurement/>

Figure 6.2 Web Sites for Working with Measurement

Journaling: Encourage students to write about the following: Investigate the time zones across the United States and around the world. Why do we have time zones? What purpose do they serve? See Figure 6.2 for a list of Web sites for working with measurement.

Millions to Measure (2003) by David M. Schwartz

(Grades 1–5) This visually appealing book introduces different measurement systems to students. Marvelosissimo the Mathematical Magician takes several kids on a hot-air balloon journey. While they enjoy the ride, he provides them with a brief history of measurement and presents different measurement systems (length, weight, and volume) and tools for measuring. The metric system is also introduced (meters, liters, and grams). This book also provides examples of the different measurements, allowing students to develop common referents.

Suggestions for Classroom Use

1. Assist students in understanding the metric system by introducing some common prefixes. For example, kilo- means "1,000"; therefore, a kilometer equals 1,000 meters. Likewise, milli- means "1,000th," so a millimeter equals .001 of a meter.

2. Allow students to compare the weight or mass of objects using a pan balance or scale. This will provide them with different benchmarks for weight.

3. Encourage students to work with fluid containers (ounces, cups, pints, quarts, and gallons) so that they can see and experience the conversions (e.g., two cups = one pint). Additionally, you can show the students different types of containers with the same measure so that they can see the capacity of each is the same.

4. Visit the National Library of Virtual Manipulatives Web site <http://nlvm.usu.edu/en/nav/vLibrary.html>. The measurement site offers an excellent problem solving activity for students titled "Fill and Pour."

5. Teachers and librarians can order the MIND GAMES CD (Earth Tone Enterprises, Item 1181). This CD uses hip-hop, rap, and pop music to teach the metric system and other subject areas.

Journaling: Encourage students to write about the following: In *Millions to Measure,* the author mentions the story of the Mars Climate Observer. The spacecraft was destroyed because of an error made by a NASA contractor. Investigate this mission and the metric mix-up. Explain what seems to have happened.

Alexander, Who Used to Be Rich Last Sunday (1978) by Judith Viorst

(Grades K–8) This book focuses on money skills, such as making change and the value of coins. Alexander feels rich when his grandparents give him a dollar. He spends his money on candy, toys, a snake rental, and so on before trying to make money by returning bottles, looking for change in telephone booths, and even trying to pull a tooth in the hope that the tooth fairy will pay him a visit! At the end, Alexander is left with nothing but bus tokens.

Suggestions for Classroom Use

1. Students can follow along as the story is read, subtracting the amount of money from a dollar in accordance with the amount that Alexander spends. This allows the students to practice coin recognition and making change. Money manipulatives can be found at the ETA/Cuisenaire Web site <http://www.etacuisenaire.com>.

2. Students can also identify different coin combinations that represent of the money Alexander spends and the money he receives as change.

3. Provide the students with a shopping list that includes different high-interest items they can purchase for less than a dollar. Next, ask the students to decide how they would spend their dollar and justify each purchase.

4. Alexander states that it is difficult to save money. Students can investigate the benefits of saving money, including such topics as interest earned.

Inform the students that they must save $10.00 (this amount can vary) for a special item that they would like to purchase. Ask students to identify different ways that they can save money to reach that amount.

Journaling: Ask students to investigate the U.S. Mint. What is its purpose? Where are the Mint facilities located? What is the history behind the U.S. Mint?

Works Cited

Cathcart, W. George, Yvonne Pothier, James Vance, and Nadine Bezuk. *Learning Mathematics in Elementary and Middle Schools.* Upper Saddle River, NJ: Pearson, 2006.

National Council of Teachers of Mathematics. *Principles and Standards for School Mathematics.* Reston, VA: National Council of Teachers of Mathematics, 2000.

Van De Walle, John, Karen Karp, and Jennifer Bay-Williams. *Elementary and Middle School Mathematics.* Boston: Allyn and Bacon, 2010.

Children's Books Cited

Adler, David. *How Tall, How Short, How Faraway.* Illus. Nancy Tobin. New York: Holiday House, 1999.

Hightower, Susan. *Twelve Snails to One Lizard: A Tale of Mischief and Measurement.* Illus. Matt Novak. New York: Simon and Schuster, 1997.

Hutchins, Pat. *Clocks and More Clocks.* New York: Aladdin, 1970.

Schwartz, David. *Millions to Measure.* Illus. Steven Kellogg. New York: HarperCollins, 2003.

Viorst, Judith. *Alexander, Who Used to Be Rich Last Sunday.* Illus. Ray Cruz. New York: Atheneum, 1978.

Additional Titles

Adler, David A. *Money Madness.* Illus. Edward Miller. New York: Holiday House, 2008. (Grades K–3)

> Adler introduces the concept of using money (e.g., coins, bills, and so on) to get things you need and want. He also suggests that people use credit cards like currency.

Clements, Andrew. *Lunch Money.* Illus. Brian Selznick. New York: Simon and Schuster, 2005. (Grades 4–6)

> Greg Kenton has always had a talent for earning and saving money, but during sixth grade he decides to make his classmates his customers when he begins selling his comic books. The comic books sell so well that Greg's nemesis, Maura, decides to make and produce one of her own. Furious that Maura is infringing upon his customer base, Greg confronts her. They argue back and forth, but, by the end of the book, they have found away to work together.

Davies, Jacqueline. *The Lemonade War.* Boston: Houghton Mifflin, 2007. (Grades 3–5)

> Evan Treski and his younger sister, Jessie, are close until Jessie gets skipped to the fourth grade, and he has to share a classroom with her. They vent their frustrations with each other by waging a lemonade war. Setting up separate stands, they compete to see who will earn $100 first. Marketing terms head each chapter, while simple math problems, receipts, profit projection analyses, and charts are also included.

Formichelli, Linda, and W. Eric Martin. *Tools of Timekeeping: A Kid's Guide to the History and Science of Telling Time* (Tools of Discovery Series). White River Junction, VT: Nomad, 2005. (Grades 5–8)

> While the authors trace the history of time and how it has been kept, they also argue that time has always been important, especially during the 21st century. Numerous hands-on activities challenge readers to use household items to build a sundial or to make a quadrant, an incense clock, and more. A list of resources, a glossary, and black-and-white photos, diagrams, and maps enhance the text.

Harris, Nicholas. *How Tall?: Facts, Records, and Height Comparisons of Ordinary and Extraordinary Things.* Farmington Hills, MI: Blackbirch/Thomson Gale, 2004. (Grades 3–6)

After the front matter, the book works best turned vertically so that the comparisons of the heights of things are clearer, as the heights of objects from 0.0003 inches (a nanothermometer) to 29,021 feet (Mount Everest) are featured. At the beginning of one page, an object may be the tallest portrayed, while on the following page it is the shortest. For example, when standing beside a two-year-old child, a Compsognathus dinosaur, a meerkat, and a lesser mouse deer, an Emperor penguin is the tallest, but an Emperor penguin is the shortest when compared with a giraffe, a man, a brown bear, or an ostrich. Sidebars listing the tallest animals, buildings, waterfalls, and mountains are placed throughout the book. Harris also wrote *How Big?: Facts, Records, and Size Comparisons of Ordinary and Extraordinary Things* (2004).

Hillman, Ben. *How Big Is It?: A BIG Book all about BIGNESS* (What's the Big Idea?). New York: Scholastic Reference, 2007. (Grades 3–5)

Each page highlights an enormous animal, insect, or object in a full-color image, along with a paragraph filled with facts. The object is shown large enough to make its size clear in relation to the things around it. For example, a little girl is shown trying to catch a dragonfly as it would have looked during the Carboniferous period. In another spread, the focus is on a googol, as a little boy seated at the breakfast table stares up at a never-ending stack of waffles.

Hoban, Tana. *Is It Larger? Is It Smaller?* New York: Greenwillow, 1985. (Grades K–1)

Color photographs displayed on a white background show small and large versions of the same object or animal; for example, there are photos of a small, medium, and large leaf and of a large pig and her seven piglets. Some photos, like the one with the child lounging on the floor surrounded by small and large books, pillows, and teddy bears, show several small and large items. A few photos (the photos of paper dolls and icicles) encourage moving beyond size perception to counting.

Hutchins, Hazel. *A Second Is a Hiccup: A Child's Book of Time*. Illus. Kady MacDonald Denton. New York: Arthur A. Levine, 2007. (Grades K–2)

Illustrations complement the text as both depict the passing of time (i.e., seconds, minutes, hours, days, weeks, and years), using the daily activities of three children and their families.

Jenkins, Steve. *Actual Size*. Boston: Houghton, 2004. (Grades K–5)

The author/illustrator used collages of cut and torn paper to depict large (e.g., Alaskan brown bear, ostrich, and Siberian tiger) and small (e.g., dwarf goby and pygmy shrew) animals. Details, particularly length and weight, about each animal appear in small print near the illustration. A triple-spread page shows the face of a saltwater crocodile on one side and the body of a Goliath frog on the other. The book ends with descriptions of each animal and its habitat. Also see Jenkins's *Prehistoric Actual Size* (2005).

Koscielniak, Bruce. *About Time: A First Look at Time and Clocks*. New York: Houghton Mifflin, 2004. (Grades 3–5)

Beginning with the Sumerians of 3500 B.C. and the Egyptians of 2600 B.C., the author explains how time has been measured through the years. People (e.g., Julius Caesar, Pope Gregory XIII, Christiaan Huygens, and Albert Einstein) who had an impact on the development of how time is defined and kept are briefly mentioned. Watercolor illustrations that depict different kinds of clocks—water clock, oil lamp clock, bell clock, hourglass sand clock—are accompanied by notes that explain how they were used, who used them, and when.

Leedy, Loreen. *Follow the Money!* New York: Holiday House, 2002. (Grades K–3)

A chain of exciting events is relayed after Lincoln (embossed on a penny) asks George (as seen on the quarter) about his day. As soon as the quarter is stamped at the U.S. Mint, he travels to the Federal Reserve and then on to the town bank and the grocery store. While in the register, he meets all of the other coins and paper bills. Cartoonish illustrations depict busy customers adding and subtracting before going to the register to make purchases. The quarter continues to travel from place to place—a piggybank, a purse, a vending machine—but, wherever he goes, he meets other coins. A helpful list of vocabulary words and information related to money is at the end of the book.

———. *Measuring Penny.* New York: Henry Holt, 1997. (Grades 2–6)

For homework, Lisa has to measure an object. She chooses to measure her pet dog, Penny, using standard (e.g., inches, centimeters, and feet) and nonstandard units (e.g., cotton swabs and dog biscuits). Lisa compares Penny's measurements to measurements of other types of dogs before deciding to record the amount of time she spends taking care of Penny.

Mollel, Tololwa M. *My Rows and Piles of Coins.* Illus. E. B. Lewis. New York: Clarion Books, 1999. (Grades K–3)

Set during the 1960s in Tanzania, the book tells of a young boy, Saruni, who earns money that he hopes to use to buy a bike so that he can help his mother transport goods to the market. He spends months saving, only to learn that he still has not saved enough to buy a bicycle.

Murphy, Stuart J. *Mighty Maddie* (Math Start Series). Illus. Bernice Lum. New York: HarperCollins, 2004. (Grades K–1)

Madeline's birthday party is scheduled to begin in two hours, but she has a huge mess to clean up before her guests arrive. Dad volunteers to help by agreeing to take her heavy toys to her room while she takes the lighter items. Once this is done, Madeline turns into Mighty Maddie and swiftly cleans up her room. While she is at it, she learns that big objects can be light and small objects can be heavy. Tips for parents and children, activities, and suggestions for further reading are included at the end of the book.

Nagda, Ann Whitehead, and Cindy Bickel. *Chimp Math: Learning about Time from a Baby Chimpanzee.* New York: Henry Holt, 2002. (Grades 1–5)

Jiggs was born at the Sedgwick County Zoo in Wichita, Kansas, where he was kept in an incubator. The right-hand pages in the book describe how Jiggs was taken care of at the Sedgwick County Zoo and then later at the Denver Zoo. The left-hand pages uses charts, clocks, time lines, and calendars to track Jiggs's development, often making comparisons between Jiggs's experiences and the experiences of a wild chimp.

Older, Jules. *Telling Time: How to Tell Time on Digital and Analog Clocks!* Illus. Megan Halsey. Watertown, MA: Charlesbridge, 2000. (Grades K–3)

While a narrator explains how time is defined, why time is needed, and how time is kept, cartoonish illustrations and speech bubbles introduce the voices of children and how they use time. The concept of time is presented on a continuum from "little chunks" (seconds) to "big, humungous chunks" (millenniums) before the focus is turned to teaching readers to tell time using large, clear digital and analog clocks. The book ends with a poem about how long things take and lists of resources for children and adults.

Pallotta, Jerry. *Hershey's Milk Chocolate Weights and Measures*. Illus. Rob Bolster. New York: Scholastic, 2002. (Grades 1–4)

A word wall displays words such as "ounce," "gallon," "mile," "ton," "pint," "yard," "foot," and so on, promising that definitions will follow. Each unit of measurement is presented and displayed, using standard and nonstandard units of measure. For example, a ruler and 12 fun-size Hershey's candy bars are used to measure a clown's foot. The metric system is also discussed. The book ends with a brief introduction to time, from seconds to one year.

Skurzynski, Gloria. *On Time: From Seasons to Split Seconds*. Washington, DC: National Geographic Society, 2000. (Grades 4–8)

Early on, humans noticed that the sun, the seasons, and the weather were all important indicators of time. The Egyptians began to notice that when the star now called Sirius rose, things changed before it rose again about 365 days, or a year, later. From there, observations of nature were used to suggest the length of a month and hours. It was decided that seven days would make a week, and devices such as the sundial, water clock, and calendar were developed to keep track of time. As time progressed, devices for tracking time grew more sophisticated, time zones were established, fragments of seconds were introduced, and space-time was researched. Drawings, photographs, and diagrams are used to show the Tower of the Winds, a sandglass, a pendulum, international time zones, and so on.

Sweeney, Joan. *Me Counting Time: From Seconds to Centuries*. Illus. Annette Cable. New York: Dragonfly Books, 2001. (Grades 1–3)

As the narrator prepares to celebrate her seventh birthday, she thinks about the significance of time and how she remembers each measurement of time. The seasons help her remember that a year equals 12 months. She also uses family memories and milestones to help her: great-great-grandfather makes her think of centuries; her mother's 10-year-old wedding gown helps her remember the word "decade"; her family's new home is 1 year-old; and her cat had kittens a month ago. A chart that shows the measurement of time, from 60 seconds equals one minute to 10 centuries equal one millennium, concludes the book.

———. *Me and the Measure of Things*. Illus. Annette Cable. New York: Dragonfly Books, 2002. (Grades 1–3)

After comparing her birth weight to her present weight, the narrator explains how the things she comes in contact with daily can be measured and weighed. For example, she measures the ingredients needed to bake a cake. She also explains that she has to make decisions about tools and units of measurement depending upon whether the item she is measuring is dry or liquid. Many of the items in the illustrations look like they could have been produced by a child, but they clearly show the measurements on a cup, for example, as the narrator pours milk into it. Similarly, the numbers on her ruler are large and clear so that readers can see that a postage stamp measures 1 inch and 1 foot equals 12 inches. The chart labeled "The Measure of Things" that ends the book indicates measurements from a teaspoon, ounce, quart, and foot to a pound, ton, peck, and bushel.

Wells, Robert E. *How Do You Know What Time It Is?* Morton Grove, IL: Albert Whitman, 2002. (Grades 2–5)

Using humor, a historical view of time is offered, beginning with primitive people observing the location of the sun in the sky and the Egyptians' use of "shadow stick clocks" and water clocks. The book shows that the journey toward creating timepieces that keep more accurate time, such as quartz crystals and atomic clocks, was long. An author's note gives additional information about quartz crystal, atomic clocks, and time zones.

———. *What's Faster Than a Speeding Cheetah?* Morton Grove, IL: Albert Whitman, 1997. (Grades 1–5)

The speed of various animals is measured and compared, showing that even the fastest human is not faster than some animals. Animals vary in speed, too. A cheetah may run faster than a human, but a peregrine falcon can swoop through the sky faster than any animal can run. The illustrations, rendered in pen and acrylic, show an airplane flying faster than a peregrine falcon and a jet flying faster than a propeller plane. Some double-page spreads have to be turned vertically so that the reader can enjoy seeing a rocket ship blasting off into space at a speed faster than the speed of sound and light flashing through space at 186,000 miles per second. After an author's note that explains how the speed of wild animals is difficult to measure and that illustrations were exaggerated to clearly show comparisons, a chart indicates the time it would take for all of the animals and objects mentioned in the book to travel from earth to the moon.

Wells, Rosemary. *Bunny Money* (Max and Ruby Series). New York: Viking, 1999. (Grades K–1)

Sister and brother team Ruby and Max decide to buy Grandma a gift for her birthday, but, before they know it, they have spent nearly all of the money in Ruby's wallet on incidentals, such as drinks, snacks, and glow-in-the-dark vampire teeth. Readers can photocopy the money on the endpapers and have fun spending money with Ruby and Max.

Ziefert, Harriet. *You Can't Buy a Dinosaur with a Dime: Problem Solving in Dollars and Cents.* Illus. Amanda Haley. New York: Handprint, 2003. (Grades 1–3)

Pete has $3.50 (that readers can count along with Pete) to spend at Harry's Store. Pete decides to spend nearly all of his money on a green dinosaur. Though he likes his new toy, he does not like the sound of his near-empty bank. With only 30¢ cents left, he begins to look for ways to earn more money to save. In order to be able to return to Harry's Store for another dinosaur, he earns an allowance, finds money on the street, and sells some of his prized possessions (six baseball cards). Throughout the book, questions directed at the reader ask about saving and spending money. The book ends with a "Money Fun" section filled with activities that discuss coin rubbing, ways to earn money, and giving to charity. The "Facts about Money" section includes a number of factoids like the history of money, the origin of the name piggy bank, and alternative words for money.

Chapter 7

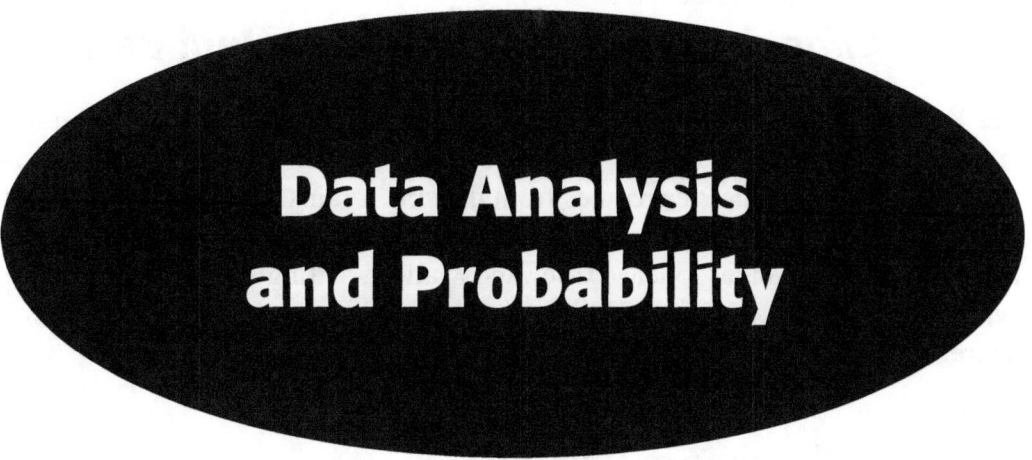

Data Analysis and Probability

The *Principles and Standards for School Mathematics* propose that data analysis be given increased attention in the mathematics curriculum (NCTM 48). While data analysis requires providing opportunities for students to read graphs, it also involves offering students opportunities to collect data, communicate those data in an appropriate graph, and make appropriate inferences about the data presented. Students must also develop an understanding of how decisions are made on the basis of the collected data (Cathcart, Pothier, Vance, and Bezuk 353). Activities should begin with basic graphs, such as bar, picture, and pie graphs, and then move to more complex graphs, such as box-and-whiskers plots and stem and leaf plots. A more sophisticated understanding of statistics and probability is also expected of elementary students, since everyday living relies on statistical information. Students must also be aware of how statistics can be manipulated and how this manipulation can mislead individuals or consumers when making decisions. Data analysis and probability activities should promote-problem solving and reasoning skills, and students should be provided with experiences to help them interpret information presented to them. Finally, communication needs to be emphasized, as students should be encouraged to question data and look below the surface of what the data are communicating.

Data Analysis and Probability Expectations

The Data Analysis and Probability standards report that students should be able to

✦ Formulate and pose questions that can be addressed through data collection;

✦ Organize and represent data in an appropriate graph: bar, picture, pie, or line graph;

✦ Apply the correct statistical procedure to analyze data and make inferences based on the results; understand probability, including the likelihood of events occurring;

- Predict the probability of outcomes; and
- Make and test conjectures (NCTM 108, 176, 248).

Using Mathematics Literature
Cloudy with a Chance of Meatballs (1978) by Judi Barrett

(Grades K–6) In this classic, the tiny town of Chewandswallow is like any other town except for its weather. The weather comes three times a day—breakfast, lunch, and dinner—and everything the town members eat comes from the sky. It rains soup and snows mashed potatoes. However, one day, the weather takes a turn for the worse, and the food gets larger and larger. Everyone decides to leave Chewandswallow, setting sail on a giant piece of sandwich bread. When they find a new town, everyone has to get used to buying food at a grocery store.

Suggestions for Classroom Use

1. Students will need to develop an understanding of the probability of an event. Terms such as "certain," "equally likely," and "impossible" can be used. Present students with different situations, such as "It is sunny today." and "The cafeteria will serve pizza today." Ask the students to classify the events according to the likelihood that they will occur, and encourage them to verify their classification.

2. Ask the students to determine the likelihood of the different events that occurred in *Cloudy with a Chance of Meatballs* actually occurring. For example, is it probable that there could be a town called Chewandswallow? Is it probable that the wind could blow in storms of hamburgers? Is it probable that there could be a tomato tornado? Is it probable that the clouds above the townspeople's heads were not made of fried eggs? Students could develop and complete a chart, Probable Events and Improbable Events. The probability of an event occurring is written in ratio form:

   Probability of Event = Number of Favorable Outcomes/Number of Total Possible Outcomes

3. Conduct several random experiments, such as flipping a coin or rolling a die in the expectation that an identified number will come up. Ask the students to predict expected outcomes and actually conduct the experiment. Encourage them to compare the results to their predictions. The National Library of Virtual Manipulatives <http://www.nlvm.usu.edu> provides a simulated coin-tossing activity students will certainly enjoy working with. Other activities on the site that focus on probability include Hamlet Happens, Spinners, and Stick or Switch.

4. Students will think the way advertisers use probability to sell products is interesting. For example, many toothpaste ads use such statements as "three out of four dentists prefer this brand." Encourage students to explore how probability is used by different advertising companies to promote products. Students can conduct similar experiments to test the validity of the statements and explore how sometimes this type of advertisement may be misleading.

5. Introduce the students to how statistics and probability are used in sports (odds of winning a game, batting averages, and so on). Students will be amazed by the Advanced NFL Stats Web site <www.advancednflstats.com>. This site allows students to explore actual data from National Football League (NFL) games since 2000, and it provides probability graphs based on outcomes of games. This site also provides probability graphs for the National Basketball Association and the National Hockey League.

Journaling: Read *Pickles to Pittsburgh,* the sequel to *Cloudy with a Chance of Meatballs,* aloud, and encourage the students to predict the likelihood of the events occurring in the story. Students can also muster their creativity and craft their own town made up of improbable events.

Tricking the Tallyman (2009) by Jacqueline Davis

(Grades 3–6) Phineas Bump, an Assistant Marshal of the United States of America, travels to Turnbridge, Vermont, in 1790 to count its citizens for the country's first census. Afraid the actual tally will require them to pay more taxes or send more of their men to be soldiers, Mrs. Pepper and the citizens of Turnbridge trick Phineas Bump by giving him an incorrect tally. Then, when the townsfolk find out that if they have a low tally they will have few representatives in government, they trick him again. Finally, the town agrees to give him a fair and true count.

Suggestions for Classroom Use

1. Encourage students to collect their own data. Bohan, Irby, and Vogel developed a model for elementary students' investigations involving data collection. This model includes:

   ✦ Brainstorming questions;

   ✦ Selecting one of the questions;

   ✦ Making predictions of the outcomes;

   ✦ Generating a plan to test the outcome; and

   ✦ Carrying out the plan, analyzing data, and sharing data (256–260).

2. Students can develop their questions and begin collecting data using tally sheets. See Figure 7.1 for an example of a tally sheet.

Favorite Sports	
Football	IIII
Basketball	III
Baseball	III
Hockey	II
Gymnastics	IIII
Cheerleading	III

Figure 7.1 Tally Sheet

Types of Commercials between 5:00 and 8:00 P.M.		
Type of Commercial	**Tally**	**Count**
Food	|||	3
Cleaning products	||	2
Car	||	2
Soft drinks	||||	4

Figure 7.2 Frequency Table

3. Teachers and librarians can support the students through each of the different stages of mathematical investigations.

4. Students can collect data to create frequency tables. Frequency tables show how often an event occurs. Students can also use tallies to collect data. In the frequency table in Figure 7.2, students report the type and number of commercials shown on television during a three-hour time span.

5. Using the data collected for the frequency tables, students can determine measures of central tendency. Measures of central tendency show what is "average" for a set of data and include the median, mode, and mean.

   Median: The median is the middle number of a set of data when organized from smallest to largest. For example, to find the median of the numbers 3, 6, 6, 7, 4, 2, and 5, first order the numbers: 2, 3, 4, 5, 6, 6, 7. The median is 5 because it is the middle number. If the data set has an even number of numbers, there will not be one middle number, so you can determine the mean of the two middle numbers; that is the median.

   Mode: The mode is the most frequently occurring number. For example, the mode of 3, 6, 6, 7, 4, 2 is 6 because it occurs twice, and the other numbers occur once.

   Mean: The mean is the average of a set of numbers. To find the average, add up all the numbers, and divide by how many numbers there are.

6. The U.S. Census Bureau provides endless sources of data at <www.census.gov> Using the authentic data available on the Web site, students can find measures of central tendency.

7. *2010 Census: It's about Us* is a program for schools developed by the U.S. Census Bureau. This program provides resources teachers can use to teach students about the census. Information about this program can be found at <www.census.gov/schools>

Journaling: According to the author of *Tricking the Tallyman*, Thomas Jefferson was a tallyman for the first census in 1790, and he had 650 assistants to help with the job. It took nine months to count 3,929,326 people! Ask students to develop a plan to determine how long it would take to count the current population (6.75 billion) of the world if they used the same method of counting that Jefferson used in 1790. Provide opportunities for students to share their plans for solving this problem.

If the World Were a Village (2002) by David J. Smith

(Grades 4–8) To assist students in understanding the enormity of the world's population, the author has created a fascinating story about a village, with one person representing 67.5 million people from the real world. Data regarding the different nationalities, languages, ages, and religions are represented, as are statistics for schooling and literacy, electricity use, and food consumption. Students will be amazed at the make-up of this village and the world statistics.

Suggestions for Classroom Use

1. In the imaginary village, each person represents 67.5 million people. Using proportions, students can determine the number of people actually represented. For example, five people in this village are from Canada and the United States. To figure out how many people in the world are from Canada and the United States, students would set up a proportion:

   $5/100 = 67,500,000/?(x)$

2. Students can cross-multiply to set up the equation $5x = 6,750,000,000$. Divide each side of the equation by 5, and $x = 1,350,000,000$. So, 1,350,000,000 people of the world's population are from Canada and the United States.

3. Statistics from the village in the past are provided. Using proportions, students can determine the population of the world during other time periods.

4. The author provides the sources that he used to collect data for the selection. Allow students to investigate other areas not mentioned in the book and determine the proper statistics for the village. For example, students can investigate how many colleges would be in this village or how many people would have e-mail accounts.

5. Students can create a coordinate graph of the village. Introduce coordinate graphing by first using the terminology "up" and "over" and then proceeding to the standard coordinate points.

6. David J. Smith also authored *If America Were a Village*. Written in the same fashion as *If the World Were a Village*, the book imagines a village based on the statistics of the United States. Topics such as "Who are we?," "What are our families like?," and "What do we own?" are presented and create a realistic view of the United States today. The activities suggested for *If the World Were a Village* can also be used with this selection.

Journaling: Ask the students to imagine living in this village. How would their lives be different? What contributions would they like to make to this village? See Figure 7.3 for a list of math series.

Series Title	Publisher	Grade Level
Adventures in Mathopolis	Barron's	2–6
I Can Do Math	Gareth Stevens	K–1
Rookie Read-About Math	Scholastic Library Publishing	K–2
Math Matters	Kane	K–3
Math Fun	Picture Window Books	K–2
Math Start	Harper Collins	K–5
My Path to Math	Crabtree	K–2
Math Is CATegorical	Lerner	K–4
Math All Around	Marshall Cavendish	K–5
Math for the Real World	Rosen/PowerKids	4–8

Figure 7.3 Math Series 3

Lemonade for Sale (1998) by Stuart J. Murphy

(Grades 3–5) The Elm Street Kids Club want to build a new clubhouse, but its piggybank is empty, so the members decide to sell lemonade for a week to raise enough money for a new clubhouse. One of the members, Sheri, decides to create a bar graph to show how many cups of lemonade they sell each day. By working with their new neighbor, Jed, the Elm Street Kids Club earns enough money to build a new clubhouse.

Suggestions for Classroom Use

1. The teacher and librarian can provide concrete experiences for the students by having them create human graphs. Old plastic shower curtains can be used as the base to create the graph, and painters' tape or other colored tapes can be used to form the axes. Questions for data collection can be formulated by using suggestions from the class about their interests, such as hair colors, ages, favorite subjects, and so on. The students themselves will represent the data!

2. Providing opportunities for students to formulate questions and collect and display data is important. Ask students to:

    ✦ Generate their own questions to explore;

    ✦ Collect authentic data by developing surveys;

    ✦ Decide on the type of graph to display their data; and

    ✦ Present their findings.

3. This activity offers an opportunity to assist students with distinguishing the purposes of different types of graphs. For example, line graphs are used to show trends over time and are not selected if a student wants to show classmates' favorite topics. The younger grades can represent their data for bar graphs using manipulatives, such as multilink cubes. Multilink cubes are colorful, interlocking cubes. Teachers and librarians may want to consider purchasing a graphing board, which allows students to design different graphs using the multilink cubes. Graphing boards and multilink cubes are available at <http://www.etacuisenaire.com>

4. *Tinkerplots* is a dynamic software program for students in grades 4–8. This software program allows students to create visually stimulating representations of authentic data, so they will be able to recognize patterns and make meaningful conclusions. *Tinkerplots* is available from Key Curriculum Press, 1150 65th Street, Emeryville, CA, 94608, (Phone) 800-995-MATH (6284).

5. Opportunities for students to read and interpret information presented in graphs must also be provided. Present different graphs to the students. Graphs can be found in the local newspaper or in different magazines. Begin the activity by asking students questions that can be answered directly from the data. Your questions should then move to those that require students to add or subtract the data presented. Finally, your questions should require students to interpret the data and focus on the patterns presented. The National Council of Teachers of Mathematics Navigation Series *Navigating through Data Analysis in Grades 6–8* offers many problem-based activities focusing on data analysis.

6. Provide students with a small bag of M&M's and ask them to sort the different colors of M&M's into groups. Using large-scale graph paper, allow students to create a bar graph using their M&M's. Create a whole-class graph based on each student's data. This can lead to a wonderful discussion on the colors most likely to be in a small bag of M&M's. The literature selection *More M&M's Math,* written by Barbieri McGrath, can complement this activity.

Journaling: Investigating how the Nielsen ratings are used to identify the top television shows will capture students' interest. Developed by Nielsen Media Research, Neilson ratings are measurement systems meant to gauge the popularity of selected television programs with an intended audience. Top shows per evening, week, and year are identified. Encourage students to create their own Neilson ratings based on their classmate's favorite shows. To promote problem-solving and reasoning skills, ask students to look at their data to determine when commercial time will be the most expensive.

Do You Wanna Bet? (1991) by Jean Cushman

(Grades 3–6) This chapter book introduces the students to chance and probability. Friends Danny and Brian encounter several situations involving probability and chance: tossing coins, forecasting the weather, alphabetical probability, and taking chances. The author does an excellent job of explaining the probability of each of the events presented. After reading this selection, students will have a better understanding of chance and probability.

Suggestions for Classroom Use

1. Each chapter in *Do You Wanna Bet?* presents a problem based on the chapter's focus. For example, chapter 1 introduces the probability of coin tosses. The questions at the end of the chapter include "What are Brian's chances of winning the toss?" and "Despite the long run of heads, will the coin land heads up once more?" Ask students to work each of the problems and to check their responses using the author's explanations.

2. The author includes several probability experiments, like forecasting the weather and alphabetical probability. Students will enjoy actually conducting these experiments. For example, having students observe the tiles used in Scrabble will assist in their understanding of why certain letters have more tiles and why some tiles are worth more points.

3. Play a game of Wheel of Fortune with your students, and encourage them to test their new understanding of alphabetical probability. You can use phrases or words based on any subject matter that is being discussed in the classroom. A spinner can easily be made out of poster board, or you can use store-bought spinners.

4. Ask students to identify several events and then investigate the chances of the events occurring. For example, students can determine the chances of having the same birthday as their teacher. They can survey friends and teachers in their school, stopping only when they find a match.

5. The NFL usually predicts the winner and scores for each Sunday and Monday night game. Encourage students to look at these predictions and develop a rationale that explains why certain teams are selected to win. After the games, have the students compare the predictions with the actual results of the game.

Journaling: Ask the students to generate a list of events with increasing levels of probability. For example, one would have a 50% chance of flipping a coin and having it land on heads. One would also have a 16.667% chance of rolling a die and having a particular number come out on top.

Works Cited

Bohan, Harry, Beverly Irby, and Dolly Vogel. "Problem Solving: Dealing with Data in the Elementary School." *Teaching Children Mathematics* 1.5 (1995): 256–260.

Cathcart, W. George, Yvonne Pothier, James Vance, and Nadine Bezuk. *Learning Mathematics in Elementary and Middle Schools.* Upper Saddle River, NJ: Pearson, 2006.

National Council of Teachers of Mathematics. *Principles and Standards for School Mathematics.* Reston, VA: National Council of Teachers of Mathematics, 2000.

National Council of Teachers of Mathematics. Navigation Series. *Navigating through Data Analysis, Grades 6–8.* Reston, VA: NCTM, 2003.

Children's Books Cited

Barrett, Judi. *Cloudy With a Chance of Meatballs.* Illus. Ron Barrett. New York: Aladdin, 1978.

———. *Pickles to Pittsburgh.* Illus. Ron Barrett. New York: Aladdin, 1997.

Cushman, Jean. *Do You Wanna Bet?* Illus. Martha Weston. New York: Clarion, 1991.

Davies, Jacqueline. *Tricking the Tallyman.* Illus. S. D. Schindler. New York: Alfred A. Knopf, 2009.

McGrath, Barbara Barbieri. *More M&M's Math.* Illus. Roger Glass. Watertown, MA: Charlesbridge, 1998.

Murphy, Stuart J. *Lemonade for Sale.* Illus. Tricia Tusa. New York: HarperCollins, 1998.

Smith, David J. *If America Were a Village.* Illus. Shelagh Armstrong. Toronto, Canada: Kids Can, 2009.

———. *If the World Were a Village.* Illus. Shelagh Armstrong. Toronto, Canada: Kids Can, 2002.

Additional Titles

Aber, Linda Williams. *Who's Got Spots?* (Math Matters). Illus. Gioia Fiammenghi. New York: Kane, 2000. (Grades 2–3)

> Kip is excited about being chosen to sing the solo during Autumn Fest, but his excitement wanes when Ms. Beck announces that several people in the chorus have chicken pox. Since they will be able to perform if at least 10 chorus members are well enough to attend the show, Kip surveys the 11 children who do not have chicken pox, hoping to collect enough data to find out if they are likely to perform. His chart shows that since seven of them have already had chicken pox, Ms. Beck needs at least three children to stay healthy if they hope to have the show. In the end, most of the chorus members are well enough to support Kip while he sings a solo. The mathematics concepts suggested are reinforced with a list of questions about a graph and a tally chart.

Axelrod, Amy. *Pigs at Odds: Fun with Math and Games* (Pigs Will Be Pigs). Illus. Sharon McGinley-Nally. New York: Simon and Schuster, 2000. (Grades 2–4)

When the pig family arrives at the county fair, they cannot decide whether to go on rides or play games first, so Mr. Pig flips a coin. The little pigs win and go on ride after ride until it is time to try their luck at ring toss, bowling, and basketball. An author's note defines probability.

Einhorn, Edward. *A Very Improbable Story: A Math Adventure.* Illus. Adam Gustavson. Watertown, MA: Charlesbridge, 2008. (Grades 2–5)

Ethan is surprised when he wakes up and finds a cat named Odds on top of his head. Odds assures him he will get off his head if he wins a game of probability. Annoyed, Ethan explains that he has a soccer game, but Odds insists, holding on tightly to Ethan's head as he showers and dresses. Odds challenges Ethan to pull a dime out of a can of coins, matching socks from his drawer, and two white marbles from a pile, but Ethan does not succeed. Ethan finally wins when he pulls two pug-shaped pieces of cereal out of a pile. Odds gets off his head and encourages him to talk about how probability can be applied to soccer. The book ends with a brief note about the history of probability, beginning with Blaise Pascal and Pierre de Fermat.

Leedy, Loreen. *The Great Graph Contest.* New York: Holiday House, 2004. (Grades 1–3)

Gonk is busy making a graph based on his friend's affinity for mud when Beezy and Chester visit. Since his friends are amphibians, the graph shows that most of them like mud. Gonk has other graphs, too, and, when Beezy sees them, he says he also likes to make graphs. After much debate about who makes the best graphs, Beezy and Gonk decide to have a contest. As judge, Chester says he will examine their graphs for neatness, creativity, and accuracy. The friends do many things together that serve as the basis for their graphs. For example, in the bathing suit shop, they notice similarities in the decorations on the suits and decide to create a Venn diagram to show the number of suits with different types of designs. At the end of the book, all of Gonk and Beezy's graphs are presented, and they find out that Chester has been keeping a graph of his own, one that reveals that the contest is a tie. The illustrations show surveys and tallies, and the speech balloons complement the cartoonish illustrations. The "Make Your Own Graph" section explains how to make Venn diagrams and quantity, circle, and bar graphs.

———. *It's Probably Penny.* New York: Holt, 2007. (Grades 1–4)

After demonstrating the concept of probability to Lisa's class, the teacher assigns a project that focuses on the concept. The students must do the following: (1) predict what will, might, and cannot happen; (2) consider an event that has a tiny chance of happening and one that is simply impossible; (3) write about two events that have equal chances of occurring; and (4) choose an event that has unequal chances. Unequal chances involves the concept of randomness. Illustrations show that most of the events Lisa predicts involve Penny, her Boston terrier. For example, Lisa reasons that it is impossible for Penny to turn into a cat or be president of the United States, and, when Lisa's favorite toy is missing, she predicts that Penny probably has something to do with its disappearance.

Murphy, Stuart J. *Probably Pistachio* (Math Start). Illus. Marsha Winborn. New York: HarperCollins, 2001. (Grades 1–2)

It is Monday morning, and Jack is having a bad day. His alarm did not sound, and he cannot find his favorite sneakers. To make matters worse, Dad is making his bag lunch instead of Mom. Though Jack reasons that Dad could have packed any kind of sandwich, he happens to pack Jack's least favorite: tuna. In school, Jack is sure he will be able to trade sandwiches with Emma, as she always brings pastrami on Thursdays, so Jack is disappointed when he learns she brought liverwurst. The day continues to be unpredictable after school, too. The soccer coach usually divides the players into two teams, so Jack has worked out a plan that is sure to secure him a spot on his best friend's team, but the coach decides to group the players by threes, so Jack does not play on Alex's team. The final scene presents the concept of probability in a lighthearted manner, as Jack's mom tells him and his sister that she brought home their favorite flavor of ice cream. Jack knows this means there is a 50% chance that she has his favorite. Jack is devastated when Mom pulls out his sister's favorite, but he cheers up when she pulls out a second tub of ice cream. The last double-page spread of the book shows Mom and sister eating chocolate and Dad and Jack eating his favorite: pistachio. The illustrations are lively, and the thoughts and dialogue are presented in speech bubbles. A list of suggested activities and additional readings are included.

Nagda, Ann Whitehead. *Tiger Math: Learning to Graph from a Baby Tiger*. New York: Henry Holt, 2000. (Grades 1–4)

T. J., the Siberian tiger, lives at the Denver zoo, where he is monitored by tiger keepers and veterinarians after his mother dies. The pages on the left show picture, circle, bar, or line graphs that illustrate details about T. J.'s development from a cub to adulthood. Color photos show T. J. in action. For example, one photo shows the staff feeding T. J. meatballs, while another one shows him looking in the refrigerator.

Roza, Greg. *Heads or Tails?: Exploring Probability through Games* (PowerMath). New York: PowerKids, 2004. (Grades 3–4)

Roza defines probability and shows how it works when one is taking true-or-false and multiple-choice tests, flipping coins prior to sporting events, rolling dice, and so on. This informational book is written for struggling readers and includes color photographs (e.g., coin toss, dice, marbles) that complement the text, as well as a short glossary.

Chapter 8

Any Literary Selection Can Be a Mathematics Selection

Mathematics Literature in the Classroom and Library features numerous children's books for grades K–8 that concentrate on various mathematics content strands. But what about those literary selections that have been your favorite for years but do not readily address mathematics? Can they be used in the mathematics classroom? The answer is yes! You can turn any literature selection into a mathematics selection. The secret is that teachers and librarians must be cognizant of the national and state mathematics expectations and standards. A little creativity helps, as well. As you read your favorite books, you may say, "There is no mathematics included in this story." The teacher or librarian has to find the mathematics! Let's explore how you can take any narrative and use it when teaching mathematics.

Using Literature
A Perfect Snowman (2007)
by Preston McDaniels

(Grades K–2) This is a heartwarming selection that teaches children about values. One winter day, a young boy goes outside to build a snowman. He uses the best carrot he can find for the snowman's nose, and he even gives the snowman his father's finest scarf, hat, and umbrella. In the child's eyes, the snowman is perfect, and his neighbors agree. Soon the snowman starts to believe it, too. Once the cold night approaches, the snowman is visited by a rabbit, a cat, and an angelic little girl, and they teach him about the qualities that he possesses that really make him a remarkable snowman.

Suggestions for Classroom Use

Measurement

+ Students can create illustrations of this perfect snowman, complete with a perfect carrot nose, hat, scarf, umbrella, and so on.

Geometry

+ Students can find the circumference and diameter of their snowman, thus addressing one of the national mathematics expectations.

+ Students can make paper cut-outs of the snowman by using paper folding to serve as the line of symmetry. Using folded paper to make cut-outs of snowflakes allows students to recognize symmetric characteristics.

Numbers and Operations

+ The snowman has a nose, two eyes, two arms, a hat, a scarf, and an umbrella. Throughout the story, the snowman gives his belongings away to a rabbit, a cat, and a girl. Addition can be used, since the young boy added these items to the snowman, and subtraction can be highlighted when the snowman gives them away.

+ Fractions can also be used to represent the fractional value of the items given away, based on the total number of items the snowman had.

Journaling: Ask students to respond to the following question: What mathematical ideas do you think about when building a snowman?

Beetle McGrady Eats Bugs by Megan McDonald

(Grades K–2) Beetle McGrady wants to be and adventurous pioneer, but, when her classmates dare her to eat an ant, she chickens out. Because of this, Beetle now believes that she is not a true pioneer. However, when Chef Suzanne visits her class during Fun with Food Week, she proves her braveness.

Suggestions for Classroom Use

Geometry

+ When the book begins, the characters are working on a food pyramid. Thus, the different geometric shapes can be explored.

Numbers and Operations

+ During Fun with Food Week, the characters are introduced to a variety of new foods, such as falafel, a chickpea sandwich, succotash, and Chinese bird's-nest soup. Students can explore the different recipes, focusing specifically on fractions. For example, Figure 8.1 provides a succotash recipe from Diana's Kitchen <www.dianaskitchen.com> and tips for using it in the classroom.

+ When Chef Suzanne visits the classroom, she introduces many bug dishes to the students, such as Chinese chop-suey ants, Mexican stinkbug salsa, cricket pizza, fried caterpillars, and mealworm cookies. Teachers and librarians can search the Internet to find more

Students can use the recipe below to actually make succotash, allowing them to work with fractions. You can also ask the students to double the recipe, thus addressing a more complex understanding of measurement and fractions.

Succotash Recipe

3 cups lima beans, fresh, frozen, or canned, cooked

4 cups frozen or canned whole kernel corn, cooked

1 1/3 cup milk or half-and-half

¼ cup butter

salt and pepper

dash nutmeg

Combine cooked lima beans and corn; add milk or cream and butter. Season succotash with salt and pepper and nutmeg to taste. Simmer for three to five minutes.

This recipe serves 12 to 16.

Figure 8.1 Succotash Recipe

Item	Price	Item	Price
Chocolate-Covered Giant Ants	$7.99	Smokey BBQ Canned Scorpions	$8.95
Canned Brown Curry-Flavored Mole Crickets	$12.95	Sun-Dried Emperor Moth Caterpillars	$10.95
BBQ-Flavored Worms	$13.99	Roasted Giant Centipedes	$15.99

Figure 8.2 Menu for Bug Café

unusual bug foods and then develop a menu for their class. This menu can be used to teach a variety of math skills, such as addition, subtraction, multiplication, and division (See Figure 8.2 for a sample menu).

✦ Possible questions that can be used to highlight addition and subtraction include:

1. What will be the total cost if I ordered a plate of chocolate-covered giant ants and BBQ-flavored worms?

2. If I give the waitress a $50.00 bill, what will my change be?

Similar questions can be posed, and the teacher and librarian can bring in sales tax and tips to address percentages.

✦ Possible questions that can be used to address multiplication and division include:

1. What will my total be if I want to order 3 plates of roasted giant centipedes?

2. If four people decide to share the cost of the dinner bill and the dinner bill is $49.88, what amount does each person have to pay?

Data Analysis and Probability

✦ Students can also look for restaurants in their area that serve "bug food." Once the sites have been identified, students can use a coordinate map to locate them. This simple activity can reinforce their coordinate graphing skills. Further, students can collect data to determine the number of their friends or family members who have eaten exotic "bug food."

Journaling: Ask students to investigate the exotic bug food that Beetle McGrady ate when Chef Suzanne visited her classroom. Which food has the most calories? The fewest? The most protein? What bug food do you believe would be the most healthy to eat? Support your answer with data.

Olivia . . . and the Missing Toy (2003) by Ian Falconer

(Grades K–3) This Caldecott Honor Award winner is one of several books that feature a feisty pig named Olivia. Here, Olivia asks her mother to make her a red soccer uniform because she does not like the unattractive green one her team wears. When Olivia returns from soccer practice, her mother is working on her new uniform. Olivia anxiously waits for her mother to finish but becomes distracted when she discovers that her favorite toy is missing. She looks everywhere until she discovers that her dog has chewed it to pieces.

Suggestions for Classroom Use

Geometry

- The selection begins with Olivia dreaming that she is riding a camel in Egypt. There are more than 100 pyramids in Egypt. Students can explore why Egyptian rulers selected this particular shape for their tombs.
- Students can use a geometry net to create an Egyptian pyramid.

Measurement

- Olivia is a soccer player, so students can find the area and perimeter of an actual soccer field.
- Students can find the diameter, circumference, and radius of the center circle.
- Students can measure any of the other areas of a soccer field, such as the penalty box and the goal box.

Data Analysis and Probability

- David Beckham is one of the most famous soccer players in the world. His soccer statistics from the 2001–2002 season to the present are available at <www.soccernet.espn.go.com/players/stats?id=8880&cc=5901>. Students can find the mean of each of the categories presented (e.g., goals, assists, shots).
- Students can compare David Beckham's averages with other soccer players' averages.
- Students can explore soccer at the Olympics. Specific medal counts of nations and players are provided at <www.nbcolympics.com/soccer/metal/index.html>.
- Students can compare the numbers of medals won by the different nations. For example, who won more medals at the 2008 Beijing Olympics, the United States or Brazil? Which nation won the most gold medals?

Numbers and Operations

- Teachers and librarians can bring in newspaper ads and/or catalogs from different toy stores in the area. Students can also search the Internet for toy stores. Allow students a specific amount of money that they can use to buy Olivia some new toys. Students can keep some type of log of how much money they spend on each toy and the total cost of all the toys.

Journaling: Ask students to respond to the following questions: Do you play a team sport? If so, how do you use mathematics when playing your sport?

Swamp Angel (1994) by Anne Isaacs

(Grades 3–6) In this Caldecott Honor Book, Angelica Longrider, nicknamed Swamp Angel, performs amazing feats, such as building a log cabin at the age of 2 and saving a wagon trail from the Dejection Swamp at the age of 12. When a huge bear named Thundering Tarnation eats much of the settlers' food, leaving them desperate for survival during the winter, a competition to kill the bear is launched, and Swamp Angel sets out to defeat it.

Suggestions for Classroom Use

Measurement

- Swamp Angel is much larger than the other settlers. Although her height and other measurements are not included in the story, students can use proportions to determine her measurements. Inform the students that Swamp Angel is eight times larger (you can use any number you choose) than they are. Students can measure their personal height, arm span, foot, and fingers to determine Swamp Angel's measurements.

Data Analysis and Probability

- Swamp Angel performs many amazing feats throughout the story. Ask students to classify the events in the story as probable or improbable.

- In this selection, Swamp Angel grabs a tornado and uses it as a giant lasso to capture a bear. Allow students to explore tornadoes. They can develop graphs that communicate the tornado activity of each state, and they can identify specific tornado paths using a coordinate map.

- Swamp Angel threw a bear up in the sky, and he leaves an impression. Students will enjoy exploring the Great Bear constellation. Using a coordinate graph, students can identify the coordinate points of each of the stars that make up the Great Bear constellation.

Numbers and Operations

- Swamp Angel lives in the state of Tennessee. She then moves to Montana because the bear rug is too large for Tennessee. Students can investigate the statistics for each of these states, comparing populations, land area, and persons per square mile. Students can also compare these two states to their own state.

Journaling: Tennessee holds a great celebration once Thundering Tarnation is killed. There are steaks and bear cakes, bear muffins, and bear roast. Everyone in Tennessee is fed. Ask students to estimate the cost of such a meal. Provide justification to support your estimate.

Chicken Soup (2009) by Jean Van Leeuwen

(Grades K–2) All of the chickens on the farm are afraid once they hear that Mrs. Farmer has taken out the pot for chicken soup. But Little Chickie has a cold and has a difficult time hiding from Mr. Farmer, so she is finally caught and taken to the kitchen, where Mrs. Farmer makes vegetable soup to help her get over her cold.

Suggestions for Classroom Use

Numbers and Operations

- Students will enjoy investigating different recipes for chicken noodle soup. Ask them to compare the different fractions used in the recipes. Students can also sharpen their multiplication and measurement skills when asked to double or triple one of the recipes.
- Students can develop a list of different farm animals to determine the number of animals on the farm.

Measurement

- Students can use their creativity to design Mr. Farmer's farm. This farm must include a henhouse, a hayloft, a milk room, a barn, a sheep meadow, a pig pen, a flower bed, and other areas mentioned in this selection. Students can provide the perimeter and area of the different areas located on the farm.

Geometry

- Students can use tangrams to create pictures of the different farm animals.

Data Analysis and Probability

- Students can create a bar graph of the number of different animals on Mr. Farmer's farm. (Encourage them to use illustrations for the number of animals.)

Journaling: Ask students to respond to the following prompt: Pretend you are a farmer. What animals would you have on your farm? How many of each of these animals would be on your farm? Why did you select those numbers?

Children's Books Cited

Falconer, Ian. *Olivia . . . and the Missing Toy.* New York: Atheneum, 2003.

Isaacs, Anne. *Swamp Angel.* Illus. Paul O. Zelinsky. New York: Puffin, 1994.

Leeuwen, Jean Van. *Chicken Soup.* Illus. David Gavril. New York: Abrams, 2009.

McDaniels, Preston. *A Perfect Snowman.* New York: Simon and Schuster, 2007.

McDonald, Megan. *Beetle McGrady Eats Bugs.* Illus. Jane Manning. New York: Greenwillow, 2005.

Additional Titles

Bruchac, Joseph, with Jonathan London. *Thirteen Moons on a Turtle's Back: A Native American Year of Moons.* Illus. Thomas Locker. New York: Philomel Books, 1992. (Grades K–4)

In 13 poems representing different Native American nations, the authors offer legends that celebrate Native American beliefs and traditions.

Thinking about Math

How is the changing of time represented?

Why is the number 13 important?

Explore patterns and shapes in nature as depicted in the illustrations.

Cheng, Andrea. *Shanghai Messenger.* Illus. Ed Young. New York: Lee and Low, 2005 (Grades 3–6)

Grandma Nai Nai persuades 11-year-old Xiao Mei to travel from Ohio to Shanghai to visit relatives. While there, Xiao Mei bonds with her family and learns more about her heritage.

Thinking about Math

Examine the geometric shapes on the borders of the pages.

Map and calculate the distance between Ohio and Shanghai.

Do Ohio and Shanghai share a time zone?

Cronin, Doreen. *Diary of a Worm.* Illus. Harry Bliss. New York: HarperCollins, 2003. (Grades K–3)

A worm decides to journal about the things he likes about his life (e.g., digging tunnels and being dirty) and the things that he finds challenging (e.g., being small and having too much homework).

Thinking about Math

Survey friends to find out things they like about being young and things that make being a child difficult; graph the results.

How deep are the tunnels that worms dig?

How much weight can a spider web hold?

How many legs does Spider have?

How much do worms eat?

How many ants does Worm greet?

Gerstein, Mordicai. *The Man Who Walked between the Towers.* Brookfield, CT: Roaring Brook, 2003. (Grades K–6)

This Caldecott Award winner is set in 1974 and focuses on Philippe Petit, a street performer, who walked and danced on a cable he tied between the twin towers of the World Trade Center in New York.

Thinking about Math

How tall were the twin towers?

How did Petit prepare for his walk between the towers?

How long was the cable Petit positioned between the towers?

Harrington, Janice N. *Going North.* Illus. Jerome Lagarrigue. New York: Farrar, Straus and Giroux, 2004. (Grades 3–5)

Jessie and her family travel to Nebraska from Alabama during the racially segregated 1960s. Because they are African American, they have to make carefully planned stops during the trip.

Thinking about Math

Calculate the mileage of the family's journey.

Estimate the number of miles between the family's stops for gas or bathroom breaks.

Estimate the number of days the trip took.

Investigate the cost of gas and food in 1960.

Hopkinson, Deborah, and James E. Ransome. *Sky Boys: How They Built the Empire State Building.* Illus. James E. Ransome. New York: Schwartz and Wade, 2006. (Grades K–4)

A boy and his father watch as the Empire State Building is being constructed, in 1931.

Thinking about Math

Why do the authors mention the number of people who worked on the building?

Make a list of the materials needed to build the Empire State Building.

Calculate the weight of the materials used to build the Empire State Building.

How tall is the Empire State Building, how much does it weigh, and how many floors does it have? Investigate other statistical information related to the Empire State Building.

How long did it take to build the Empire State Building?

If the building's height increased by four and a half stories each week, how many stories were built between June and November?

On March 18, 1931, the Empire State Building was the tallest building in the world. How tall is the tallest building in the world today?

Johnson, Angela. *Just Like Josh Gibson.* Illus. Beth Peck. New York: Simon and Schuster, 2004. (Grades K–3)

A young girl tells about her grandmother's childhood dream of playing baseball like Negro League player Josh Gibson. Her father taught her to play, and she even got the opportunity to play with her cousin's team, the Maple Grove All-Stars, during the 1940s, a time when girls did not have teams. An author's note includes a biographical sketch of Gibson.

Thinking about Math

If Gibson really hit the ball from Pittsburgh to Philadelphia, how far would the ball travel?

Once at bat, how many yards did Grandma hit the ball?

What was Josh Gibson's batting average?

How old would Gibson have been if he had been alive when he was inducted into the Hall of Fame?

———. *Those Building Men.* Illus. Barry Moser. New York: Blue Sky, 2001. (Grades 2–5)

This book celebrates the large number of people who helped build the buildings, railroads, and bridges we enjoy today.

Thinking about Math

Look for statistics on the number of buildings completed during the 1800s, the number of women and children who might have helped build them, the number of racial and ethnic groups represented among the workers involved, and the number of those buildings that still exist today.

Think about the measurements needed to build the canals and towers referred to in the book.

Consider constructing a building out of household items like straws, pipe cleaners, or popsicle sticks.

Lindsey, Kathleen D. *Sweet Potato Pie.* Illus. Charlotte Riley-Webb. New York: Lee and Low, 2003. (Grades K–4)

Sadie's family has several problems. First, the land is so dry that sweet potatoes are the only crop they can harvest. Second, they do not have the $75 they need to pay the bank so that they can keep their farm. While the family struggles to find a solution to its problems, Mama tries to help by serving sweet potato pie. Suddenly, she gets an idea: the family will make sweet potato pies and sell them at the Harvest Celebration.

Thinking about Math

Estimate the number of pies the family must sell to earn $75.00, the quantity of ingredients needed to make a large number of pies, and the number of pies that might fit in the wagon along with the five children.

Chart the progress the family makes toward earning the money it needs (see Figure 8.3).

What are the odds that there will be a demand for the family's pies?

How likely is it that Mama's pies will win a blue ribbon?

Record the tasks completed toward meet the family's goal.

List the animals and other resources needed to help the family carry out its plan (e.g., cow, chicken, goat).

Think about measurement and fractions while looking at Mama's recipe for sweet potato pie filling and crust at the back of the book.

The family in *Sweet Potato Pie* (2003) by Kathleen D. Lindsey has to work hard to help Mama develop her business.	
Family Members	**Tasks**
Papa and two sons	Fixing the wagon
Sadie and Jake	Milking the cow
Sadie	Gathering eggs
Papa	Carrying potatoes
Children	Churning butter
Mama	Adding spices and beating the filling
The entire family	Loading the wagon

Figure 8.3 Charting the Family's Progress

Nakagawa, Chihiro. *Who Made This Cake?* Illus. Junji Koyose. Asheville, NC: Front Street, 2008. (Grades K–2)

More than 100 tiny people climb on hydraulic shovels, excavators, and flatbed dump trucks in order to make a birthday cake for a toddler.

Thinking about Math

Consider size perception: How tall are the construction workers? Are the eggs and strawberries as large as they seem?

Create a recipe for the cake.

Estimate the number of people the cake might serve.

Park, Frances, and Ginger Park. *The Have a Good Day Cafe.* Illus. Katherine Potter. New York: Lee and Low, 2005. (Grades 1–3)

Mike tries to keep his grandmother, who has recently come to the United States from Korea, busy while his parents sell pizza and hot dogs from a cart on a busy city street. Worried the business is losing money, Mike and Grandma begin to successfully market Korean dishes.

Thinking about Math

Estimate the age difference between Mike and his parents, Mike and his grandmother, and Mike's grandmother and his parents.

Record the types of foods each small business owner in the illustrations serve.

Estimate the amount of money Mike's family loses when new businesses set up nearby.

Poll the class to determine which foods other students would like to see Mike's family add to the menu.

O'Neill, Alexis. *Estela's Swap.* Illus. Enrique O. Sanchez. New York: Lee and Low, 2002. (Grades K–2)

Estela goes with her father and brother to a swap meet because she hopes to sell her music box to earn enough money to pay for dance lessons. No one seems to want to buy the music box for her asking price, so Estela wanders over to a nearby vendor and admires a skirt she is sewing. When a strong wind blows, paper flowers that the vendor hoped to sell are strewn about. To cheer her up, Estela gives the woman her music box, and the woman decides to give Estela the skirt. Estela does not earn any money, but she does make a friend.

Thinking about Math

How does Estela plan to earn money?

What price does Estela place on the music box?

When Papa bargains for the hubcap, how much money does he try to save?

How much money would Estela have lost if she had sold the music box for the price the two customers offer?

Reid, Margarette S. *A String of Beads.* Illus. Ashley Wolff. New York: Dutton, 1997. (Grades K–4)

A young girl describes how she and her grandmother use different kinds of beads to make necklaces. The book ends with information about beading.

Thinking about Math

Choose a single page in the book and count the beads.

How many different shapes are shown on a single page?

Record the various ways the characters sort beads.

Make a list of the different things beads are made from.

Observe the patterns in the necklaces shown.

Investigate how beads were used as currency.

Smith, Charles R., Jr. *Hoop Kings: Poems.* Cambridge, MA: Candlewick, 2004. (Grades 3–8)

This collection of poems features 12 contemporary NBA basketball stars. The author has also published a companion book featuring superstars of the WNBA, titled *Hoop Queens* (2003).

Thinking about Math

Investigate player statistics (e.g. rebounds, assists, blocked shots, steals, minutes played per game).

Investigate player's physical characteristics (e.g., height and weight).

Investigate team averages, wins, losses, championships, and so on.

How many points are free throws worth?

How many points do you get if you score a standard basket?

Smith, Cynthia Leitich. *Jingle Dancer.* Illus. Cornelius Van Wright and Ying-Hwa Hu. New York: HarperCollins, 2000. (Grades K–3)

Jenna, a Muscogee girl growing up in Oklahoma, visits family members and friends in order to collect the four rows of jingles she needs to make her dress sing during the upcoming powwow. An author's note provides information about Jenna's culture, followed by a short glossary.

Thinking about Math

Reflect on Smith's use of the number four and other patterns throughout the story.

Make a chart of the reasons Jenna's family members and friends give her for not being able to dance at the powwow.

About how many jingles does Jenna need to make one row?

How does Smith let the reader know how much time has passed between Jenna's visits to relatives?

What kinds of words does Smith use to describe direction?

Woodson, Jacqueline. *Show Way.* Illus. Hudson Talbott. New York: Penguin. (Grades K–5)

Based on Woodson's own great-grandmother Soonie, the story explains how several generations of women have lived from the era of slavery to contemporary times. Quilting is one of the threads that connects the women across generations.

Thinking about Math

Observe the geometrical shapes in the illustrations, beginning with the diamond-shaped die-cut on the cover.

Consider the patterns in the illustrations.

Notice how fabric, words, and articles are stitched together.

Examine the directions and maps embedded in the quilts.

How much fabric would it take to make quilts like those in the illustrations?

Estimate the amount of time that passes during the span of the book.

Appendix

Figure 1 Base-10 Blocks
From *Mathematics in the K–8 Classroom and Library* by Sueanne McKinney and KaaVonia Hinton. Santa Barbara, CA: Linworth. Copyright © 2010.

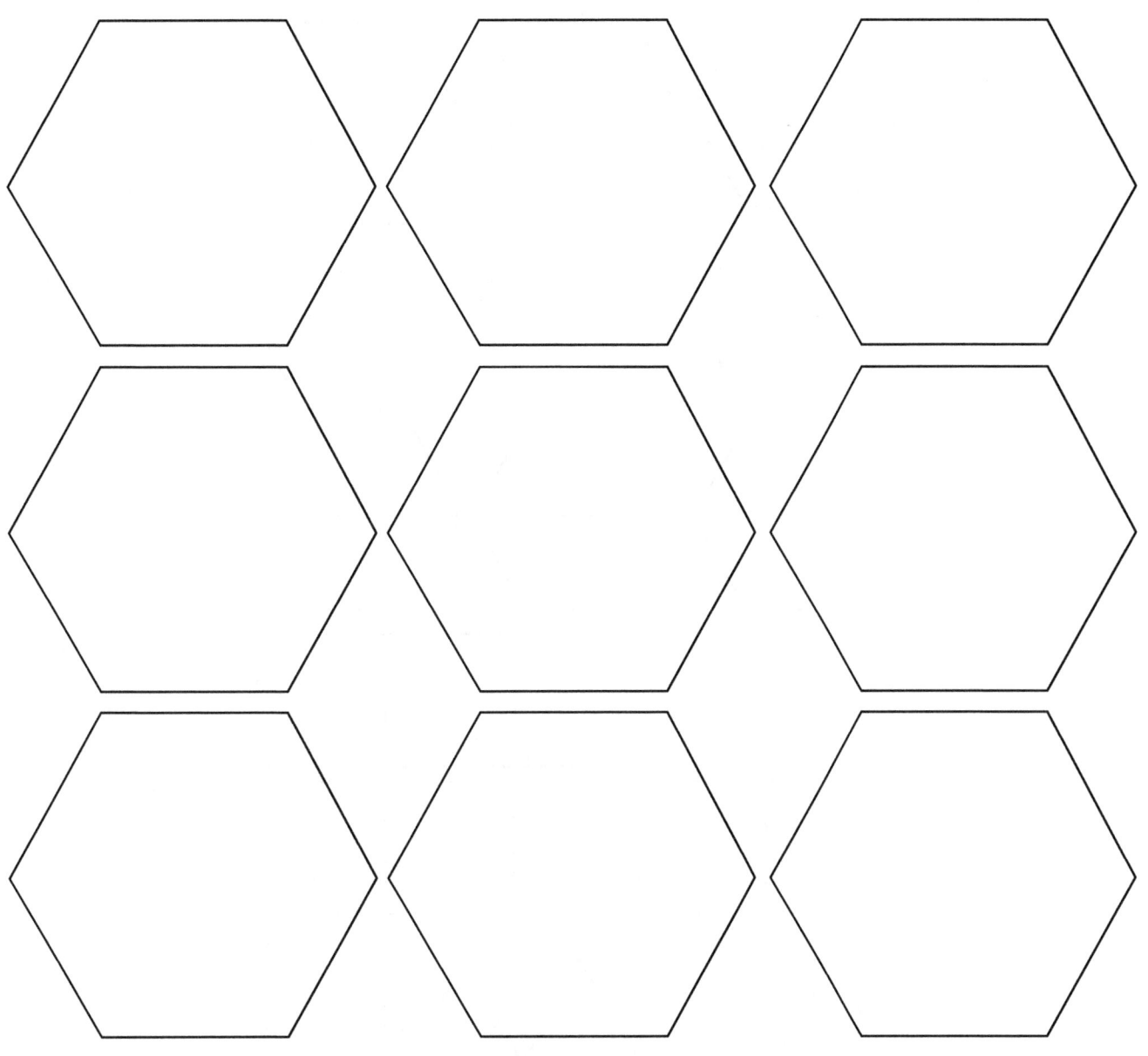

Figure 2 Hexagon Blocks
From *Mathematics in the K–8 Classroom and Library* by Sueanne McKinney and KaaVonia Hinton. Santa Barbara, CA: Linworth. Copyright © 2010.

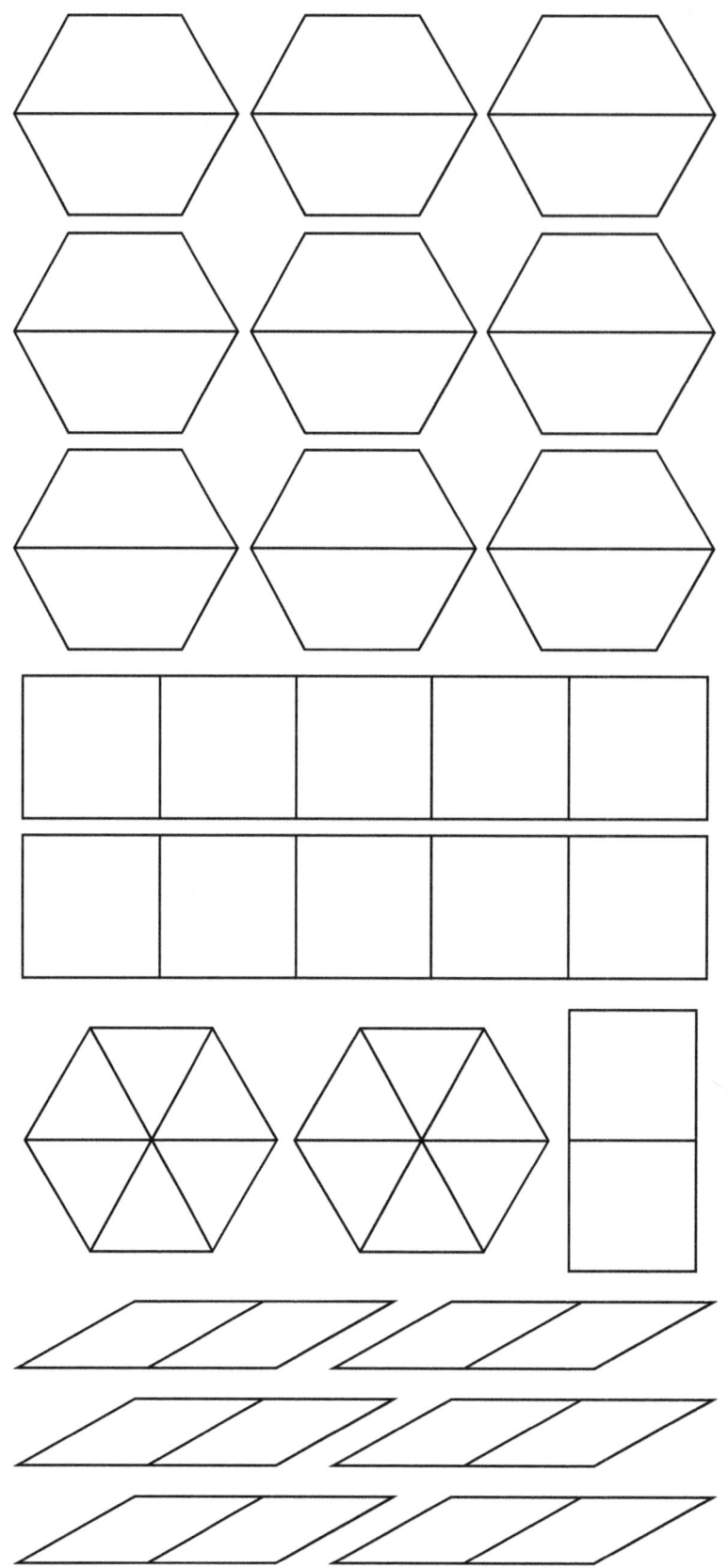

Figure 3 Pattern Blocks
From *Mathematics in the K–8 Classroom and Library* by Sueanne McKinney and KaaVonia Hinton. Santa Barbara, CA: Linworth. Copyright © 2010.

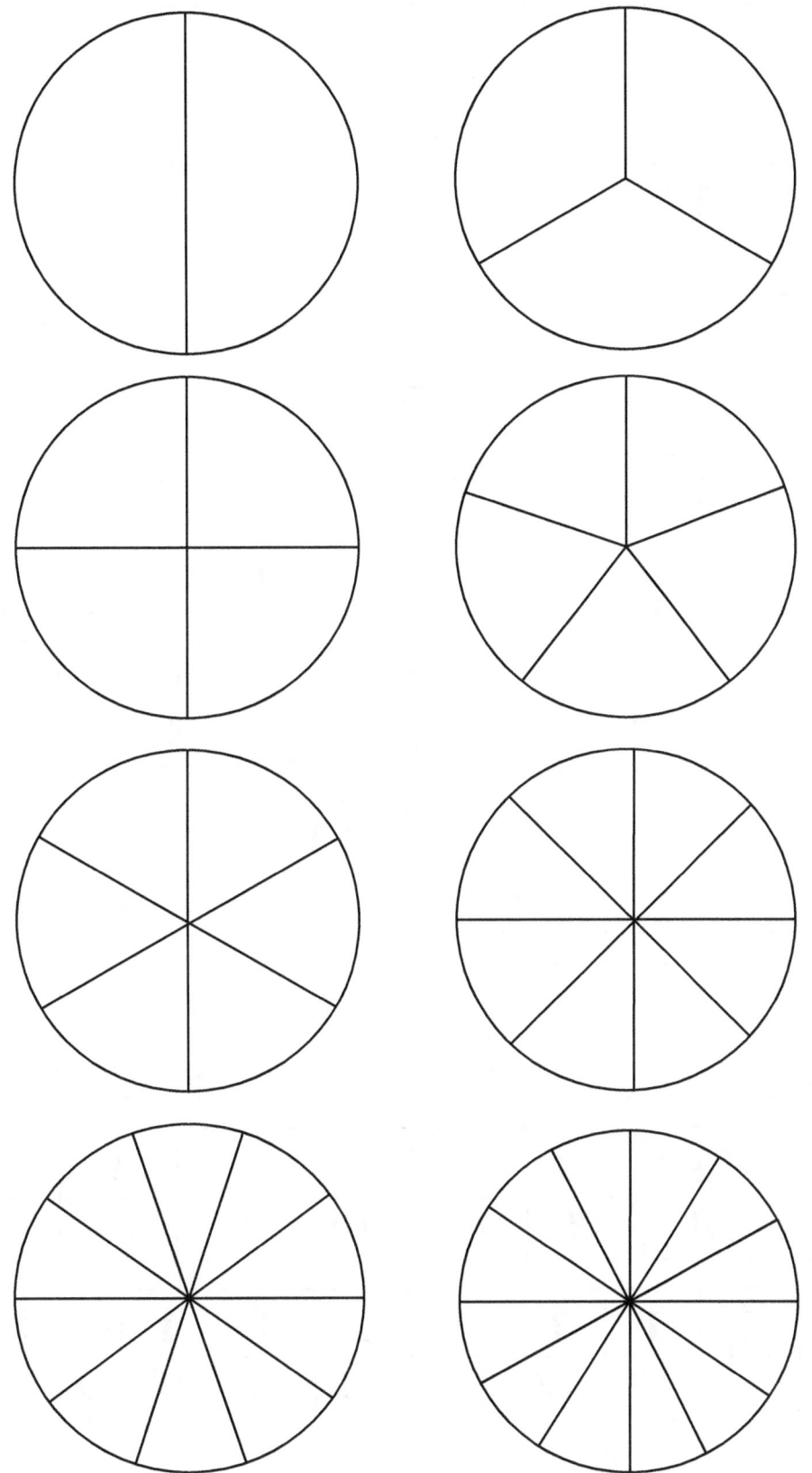

Figure 4 Fraction Circles
From *Mathematics in the K–8 Classroom and Library* by Sueanne McKinney and KaaVonia Hinton. Santa Barbara, CA: Linworth. Copyright © 2010.

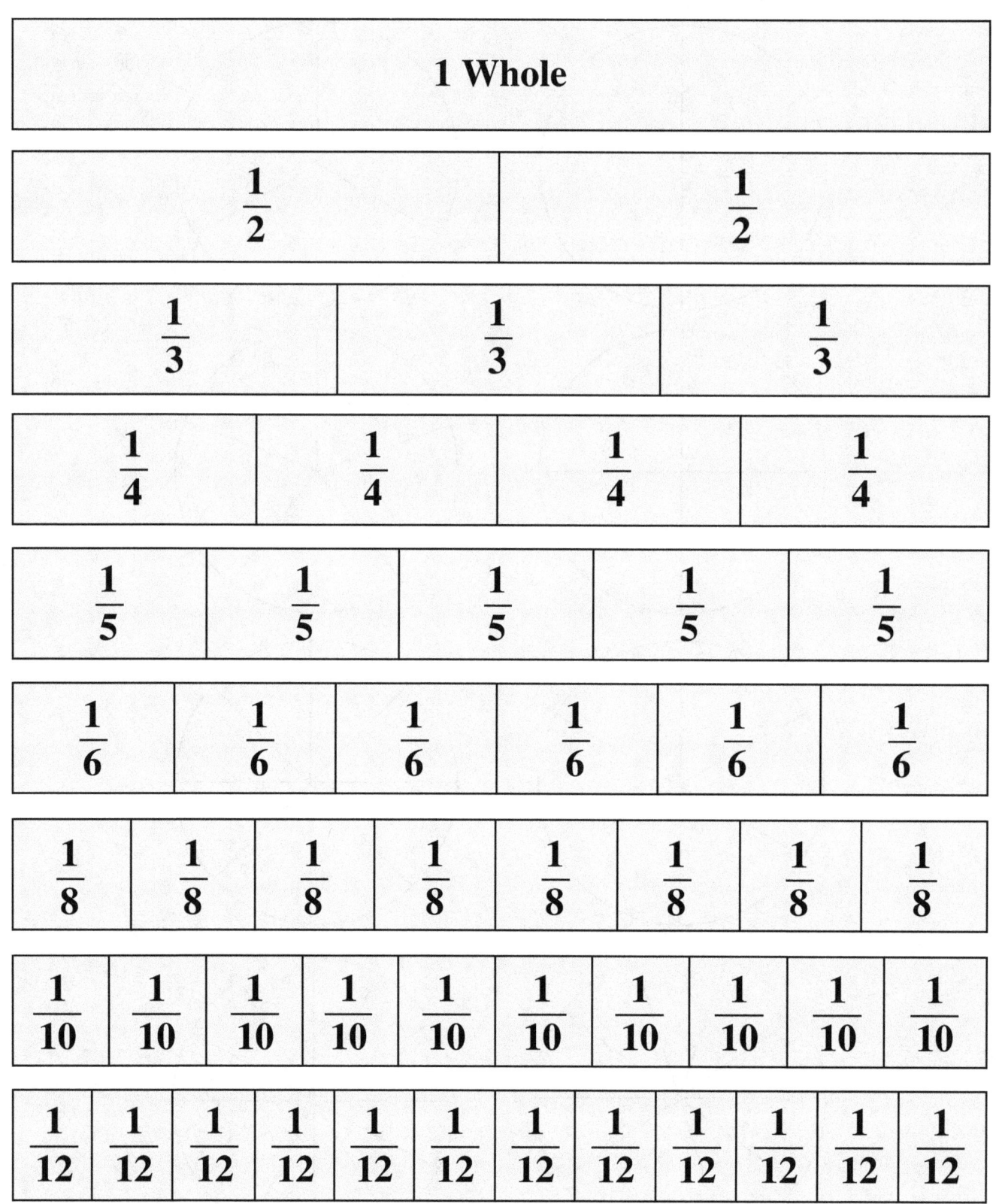

Figure 5 Fraction Strips
From *Mathematics in the K–8 Classroom and Library* by Sueanne McKinney and KaaVonia Hinton. Santa Barbara, CA: Linworth. Copyright © 2010.

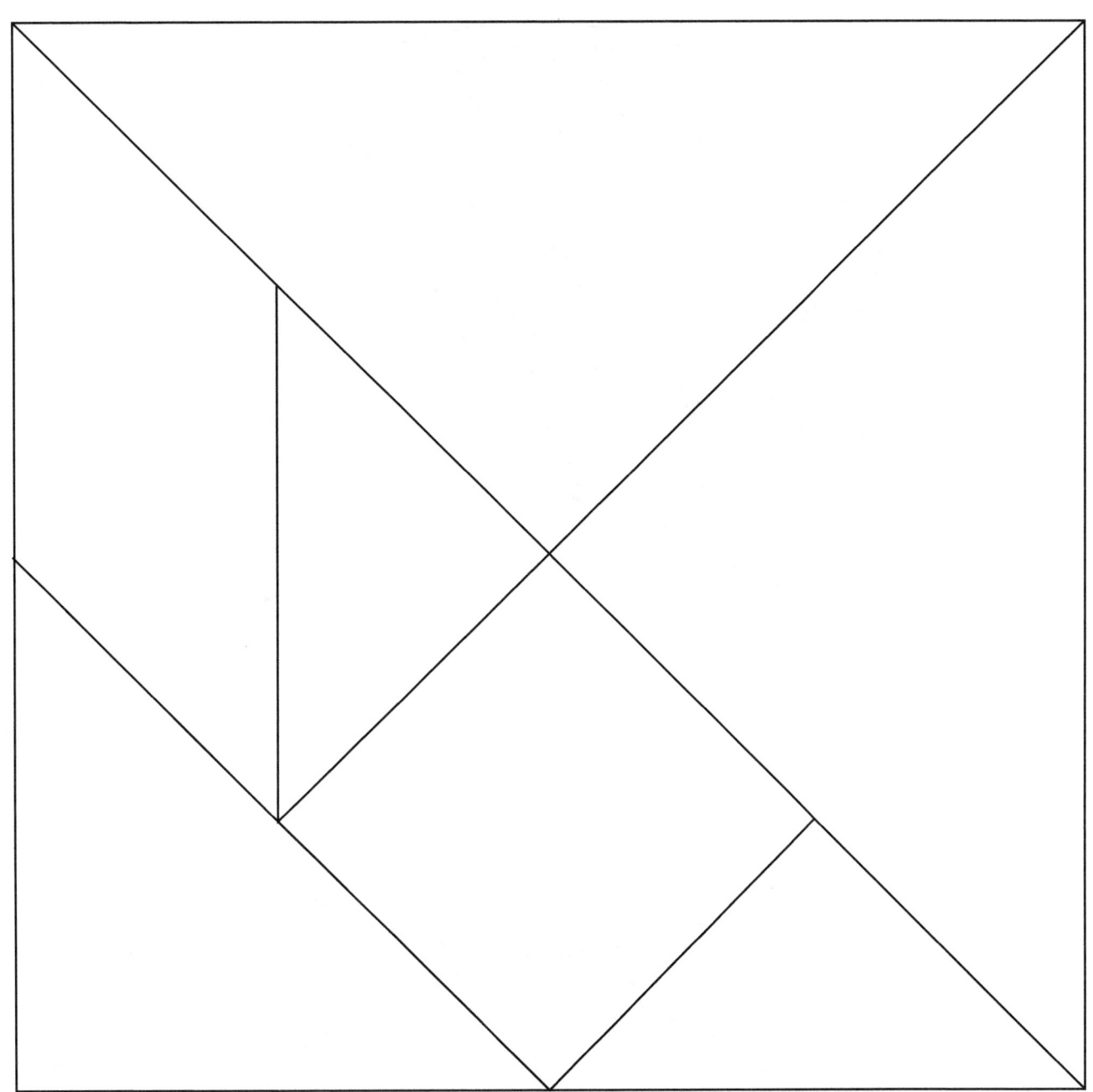

Figure 6 Tangram Pattern
From *Mathematics in the K–8 Classroom and Library* by Sueanne McKinney and KaaVonia Hinton. Santa Barbara, CA: Linworth. Copyright © 2010.

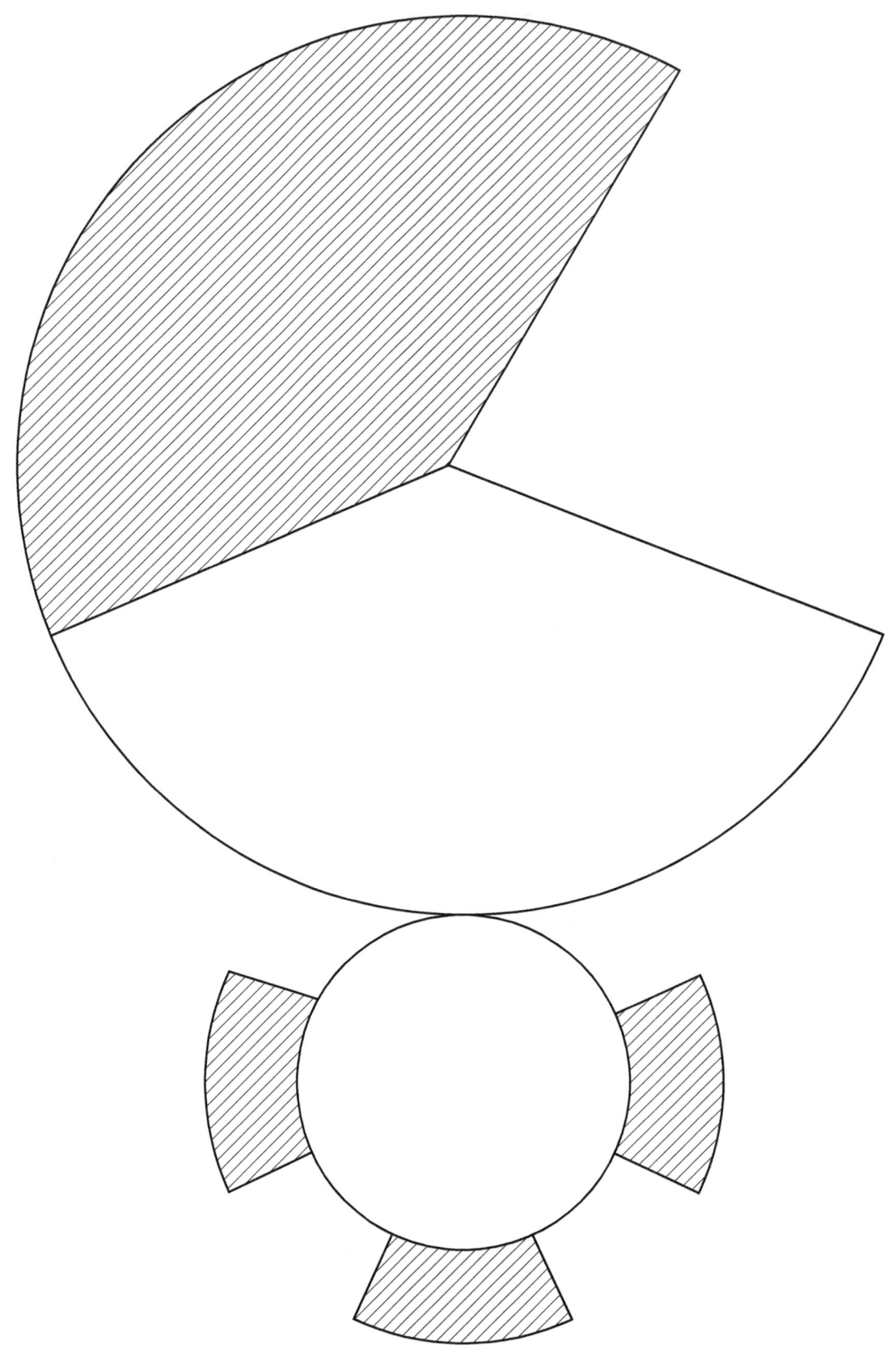

Figure 7 Cone
From *Mathematics in the K–8 Classroom and Library* by Sueanne McKinney and KaaVonia Hinton. Santa Barbara, CA: Linworth. Copyright © 2010.

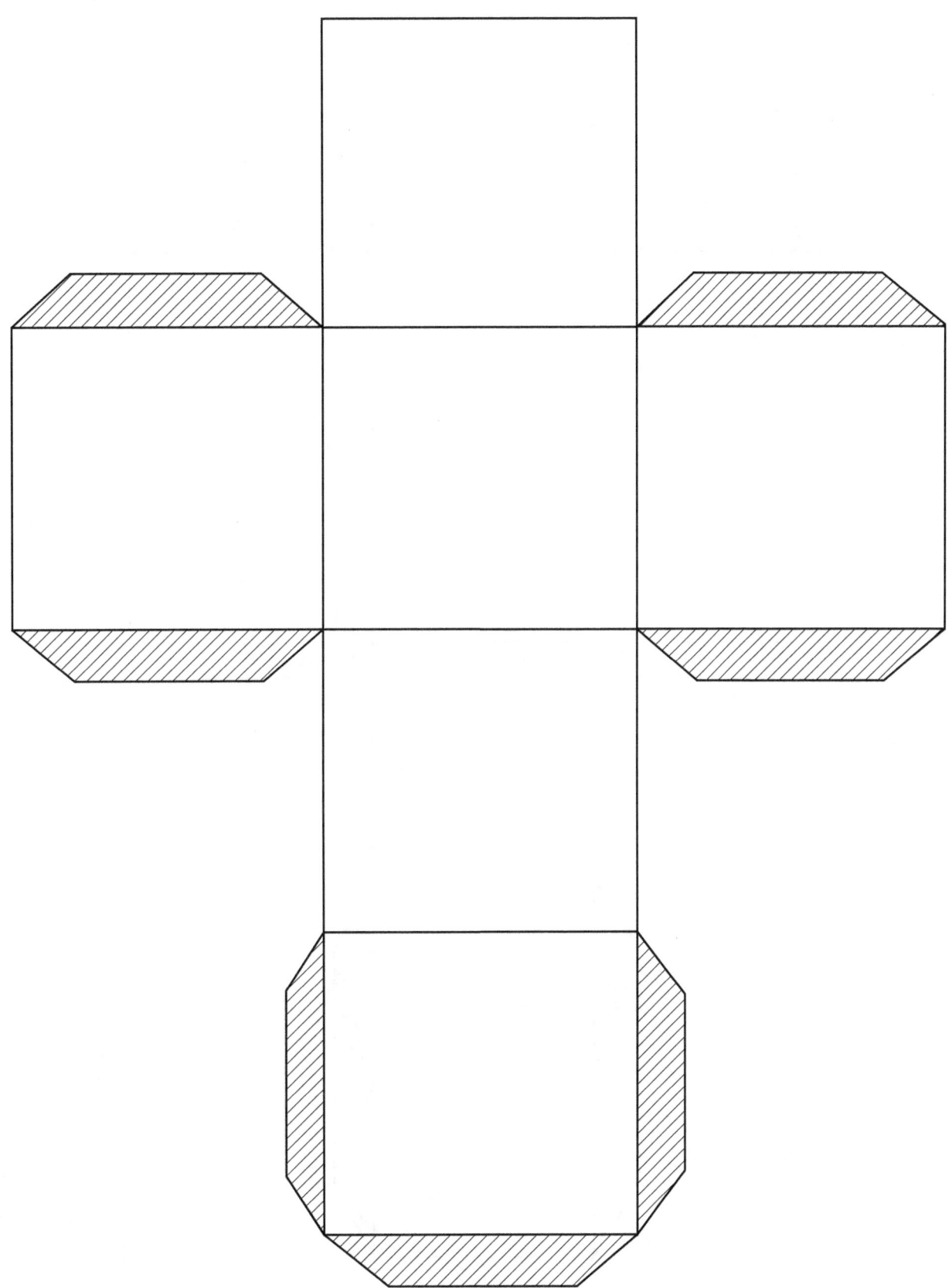

Figure 8 Cube
From *Mathematics in the K–8 Classroom and Library* by Sueanne McKinney and KaaVonia Hinton. Santa Barbara, CA: Linworth. Copyright © 2010.

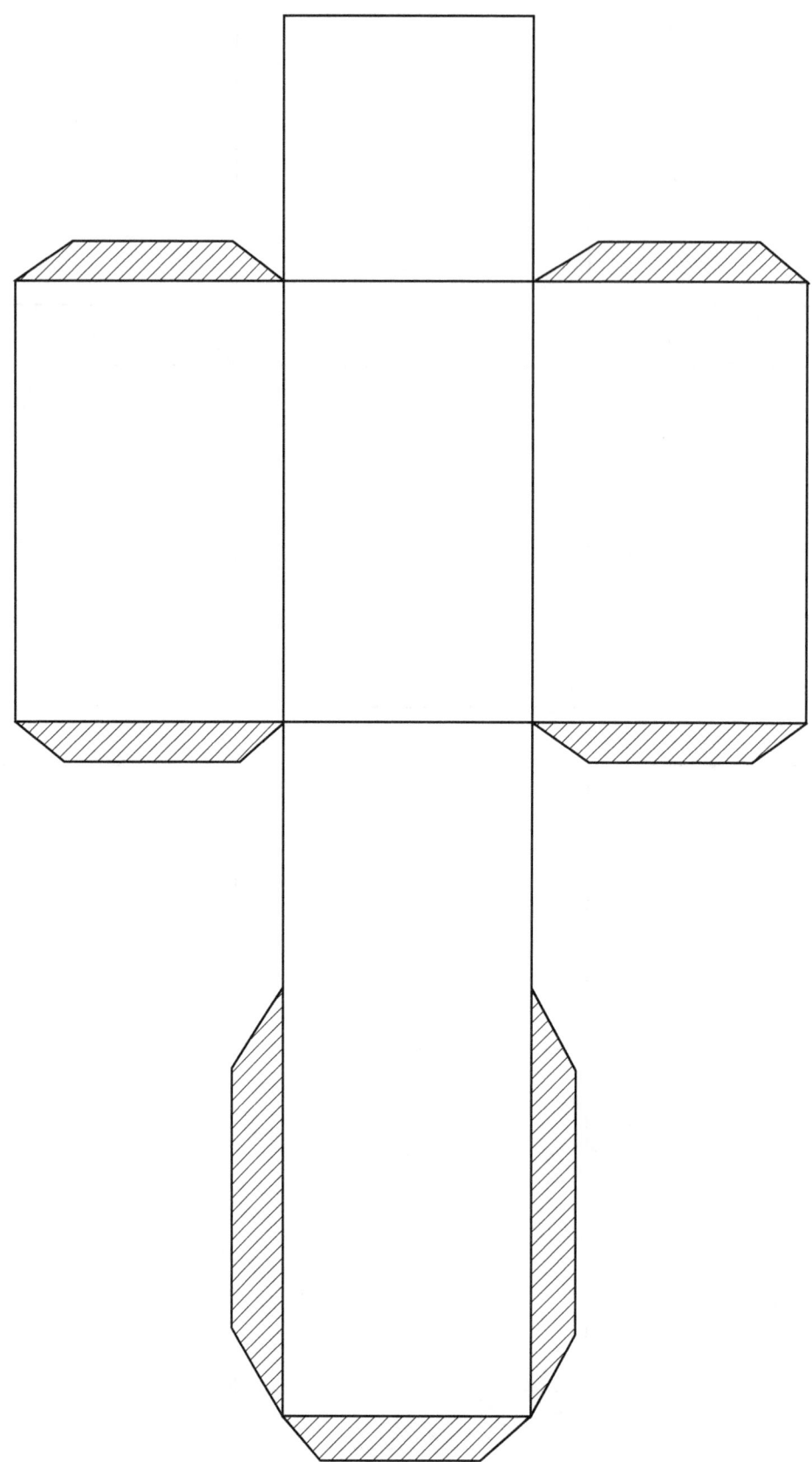

Figure 9 Cuboid
From *Mathematics in the K–8 Classroom and Library* by Sueanne McKinney and KaaVonia Hinton. Santa Barbara, CA: Linworth. Copyright © 2010.

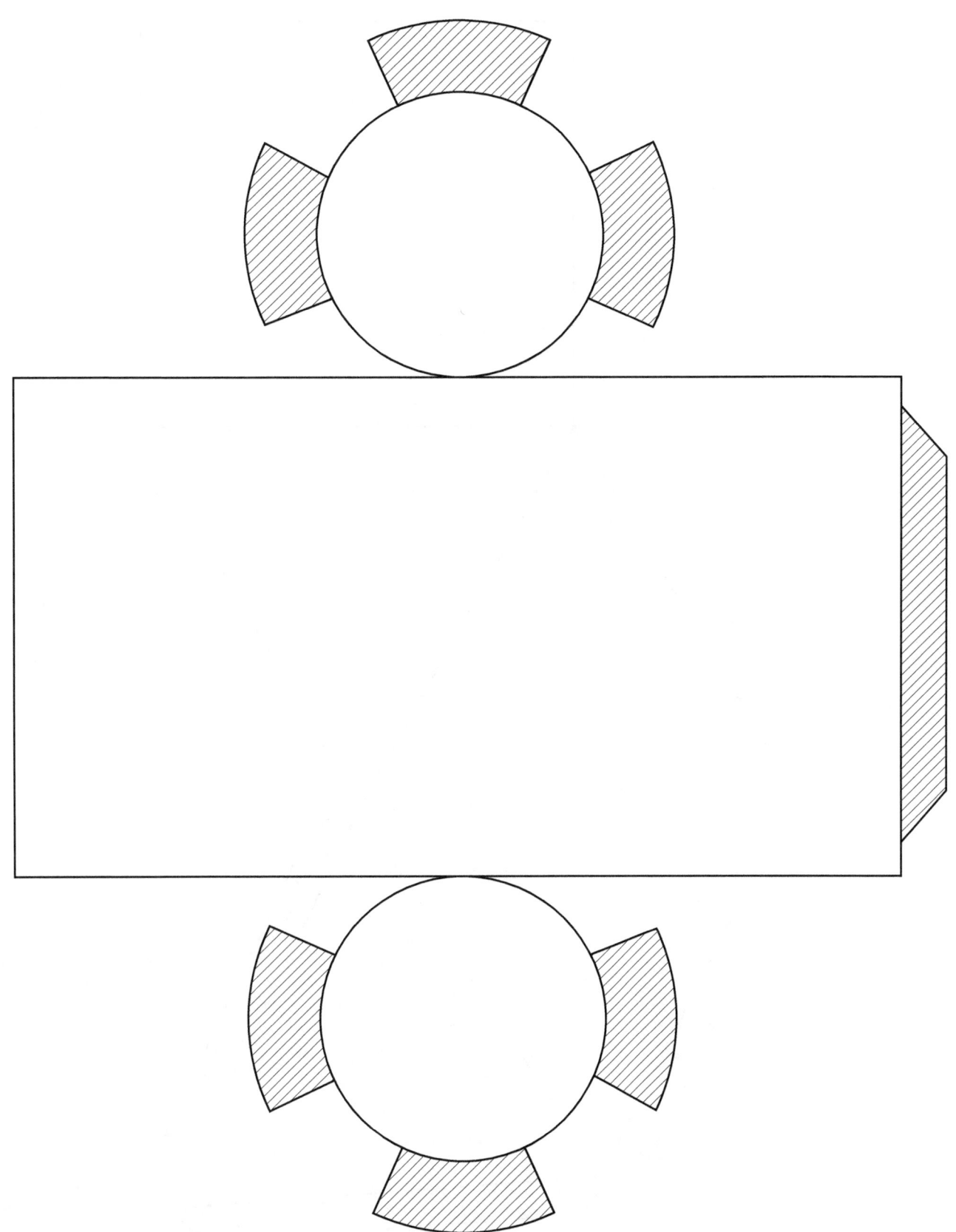

Figure 10 Cylinder
From *Mathematics in the K–8 Classroom and Library* by Sueanne McKinney and KaaVonia Hinton. Santa Barbara, CA: Linworth. Copyright © 2010.

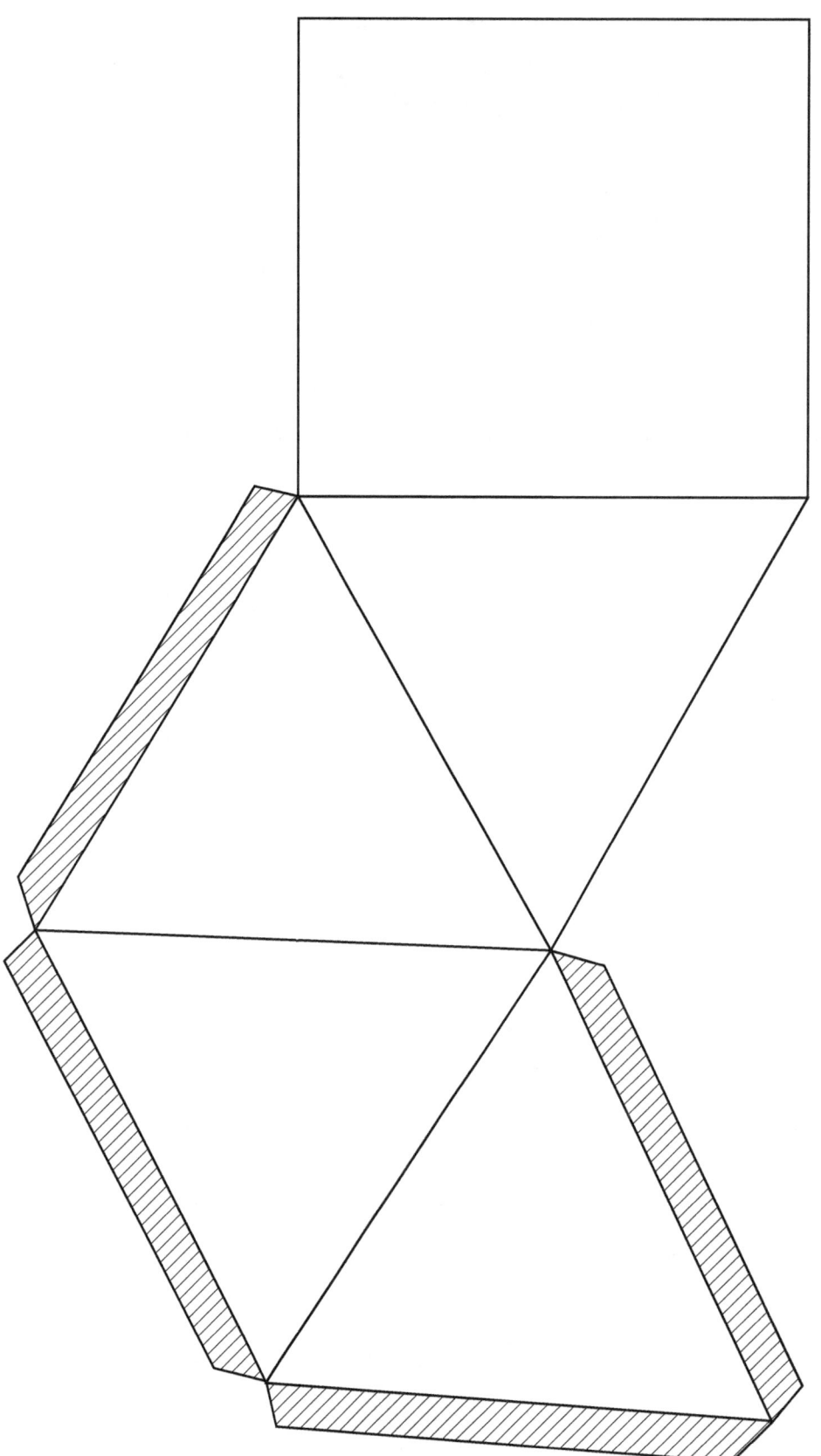

Figure 11 Pyramid
From *Mathematics in the K–8 Classroom and Library* by Sueanne McKinney and KaaVonia Hinton. Santa Barbara, CA: Linworth. Copyright © 2010.

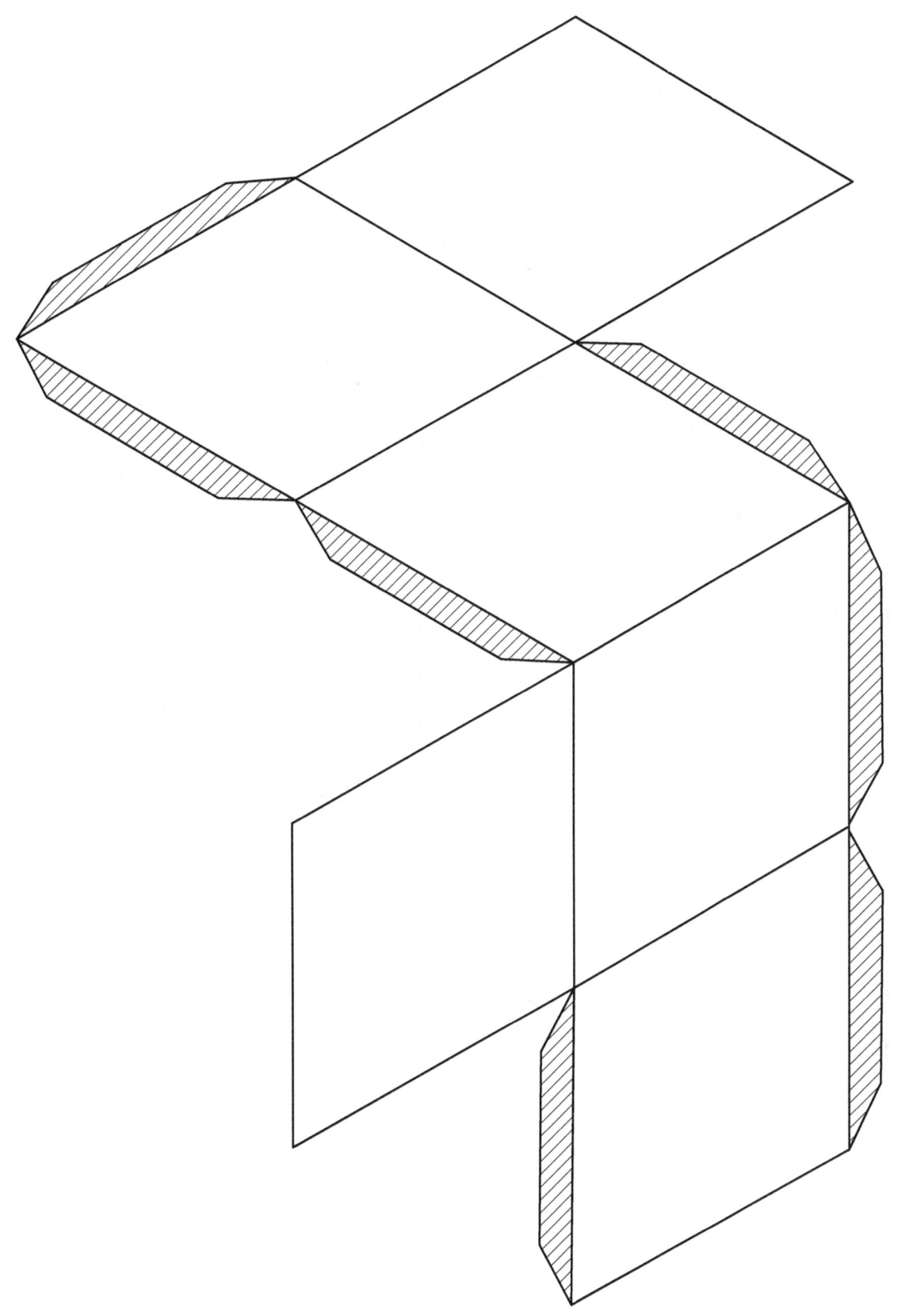

Figure 12 Rhomboid
From *Mathematics in the K–8 Classroom and Library* by Sueanne McKinney and KaaVonia Hinton. Santa Barbara, CA: Linworth. Copyright © 2010.

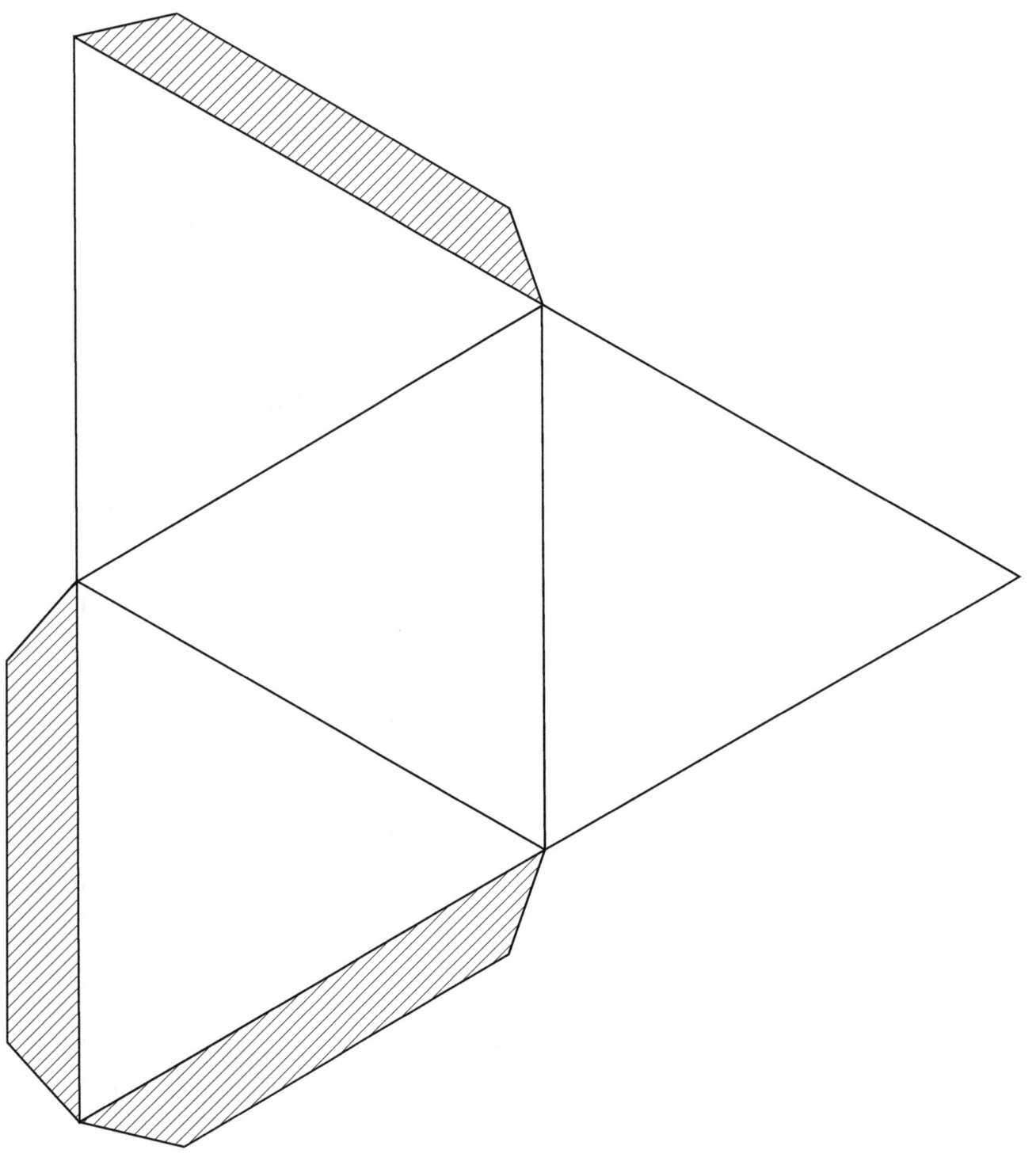

Figure 13 Tetrahedron
From *Mathematics in the K–8 Classroom and Library* by Sueanne McKinney and KaaVonia Hinton. Santa Barbara, CA: Linworth. Copyright © 2010.

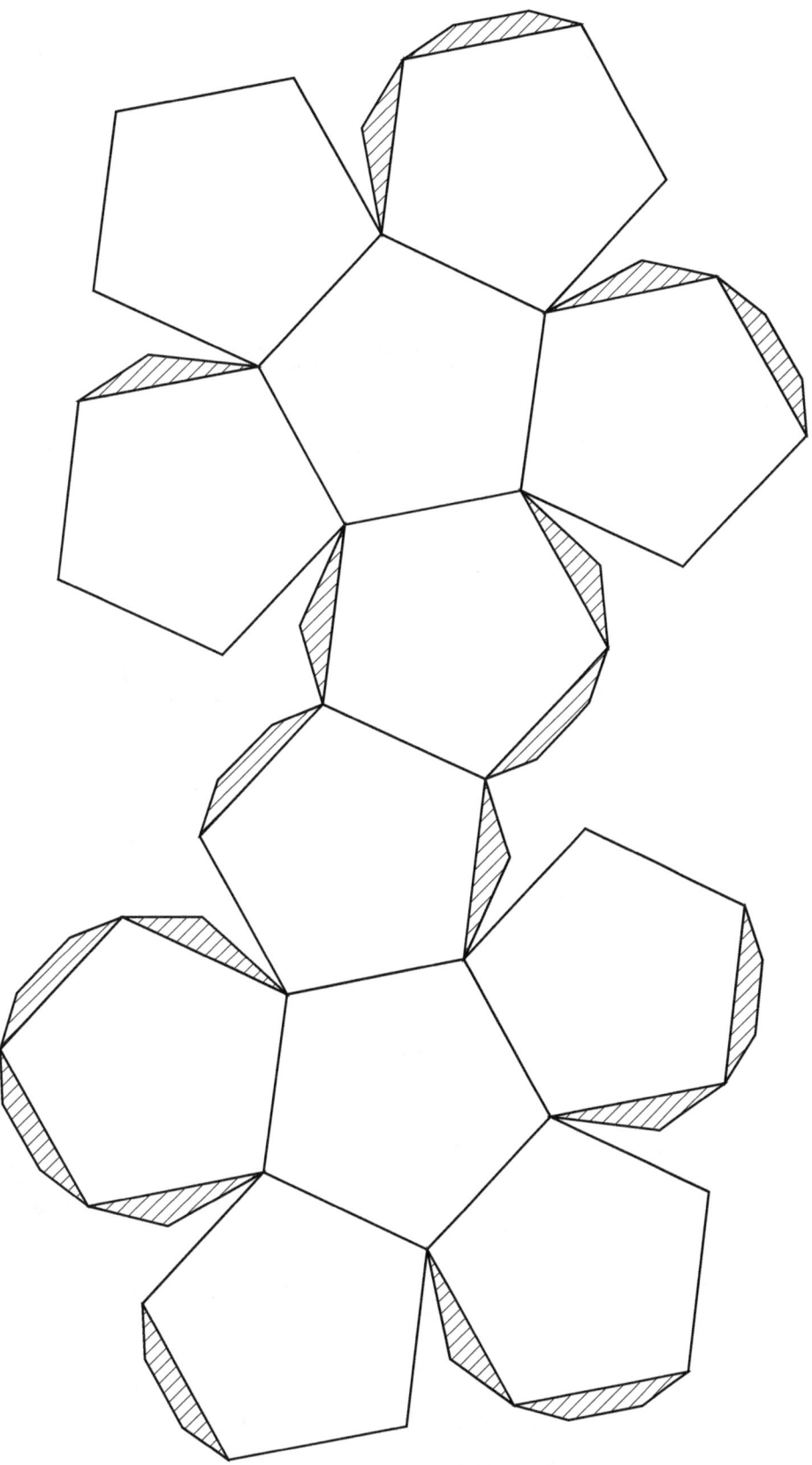

Figure 14 Dodecahedron
From *Mathematics in the K–8 Classroom and Library* by Sueanne McKinney and KaaVonia Hinton. Santa Barbara, CA: Linworth. Copyright © 2010.

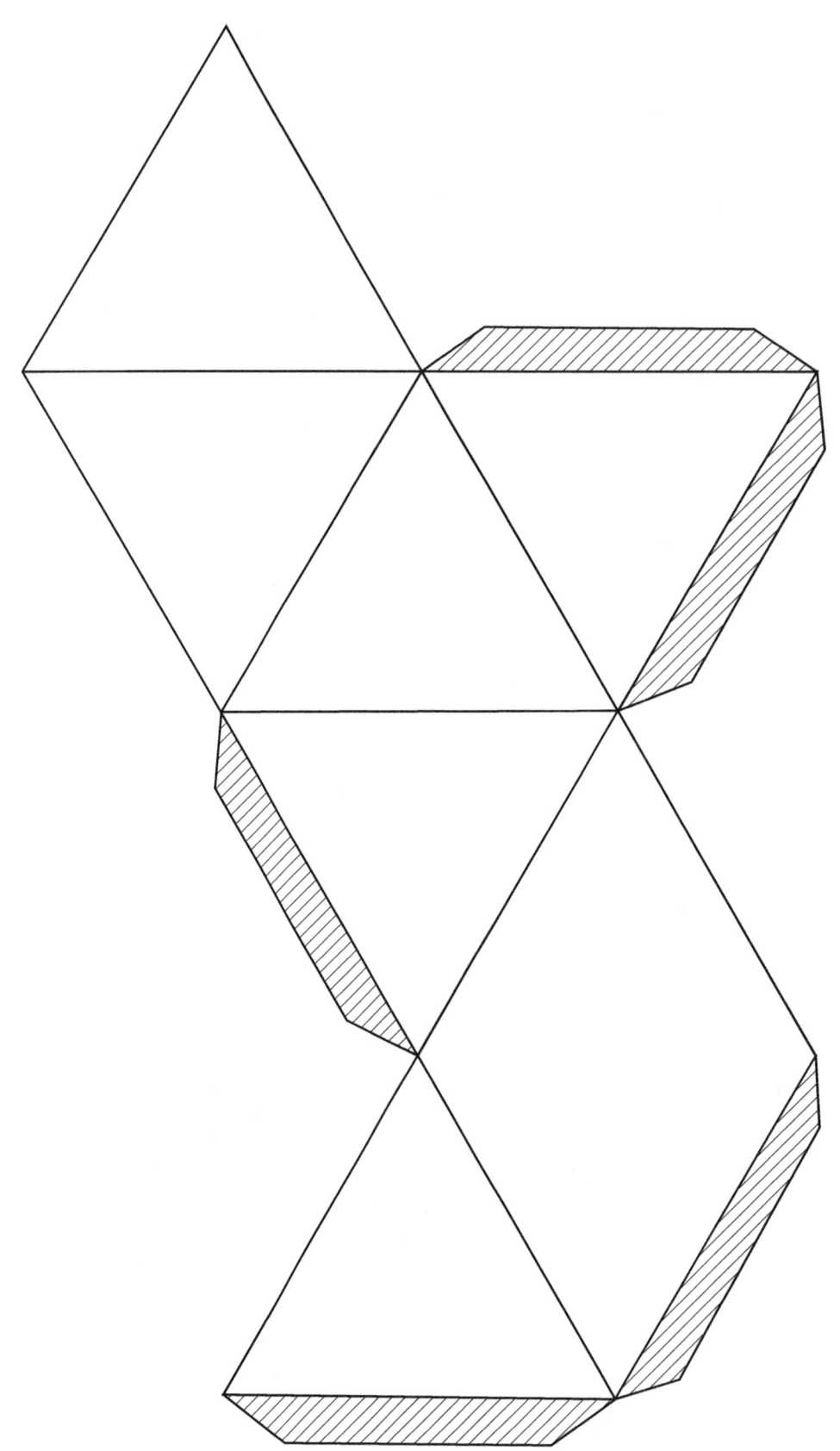

Figure 15 Octahedron
From *Mathematics in the K–8 Classroom and Library* by Sueanne McKinney and KaaVonia Hinton. Santa Barbara, CA: Linworth. Copyright © 2010.

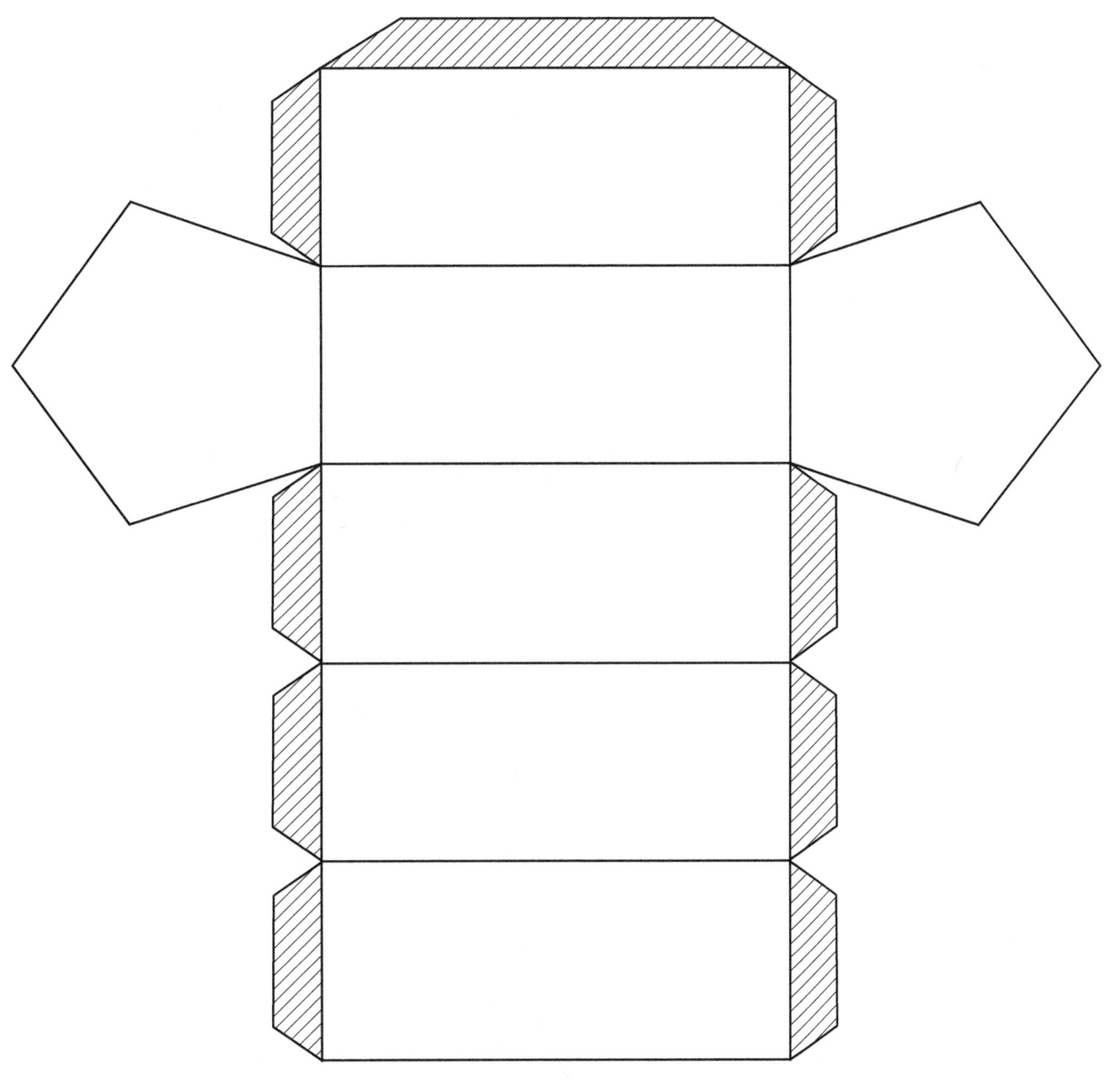

Figure 16 Pentagon Prism
From *Mathematics in the K–8 Classroom and Library* by Sueanne McKinney and KaaVonia Hinton. Santa Barbara, CA: Linworth. Copyright © 2010.

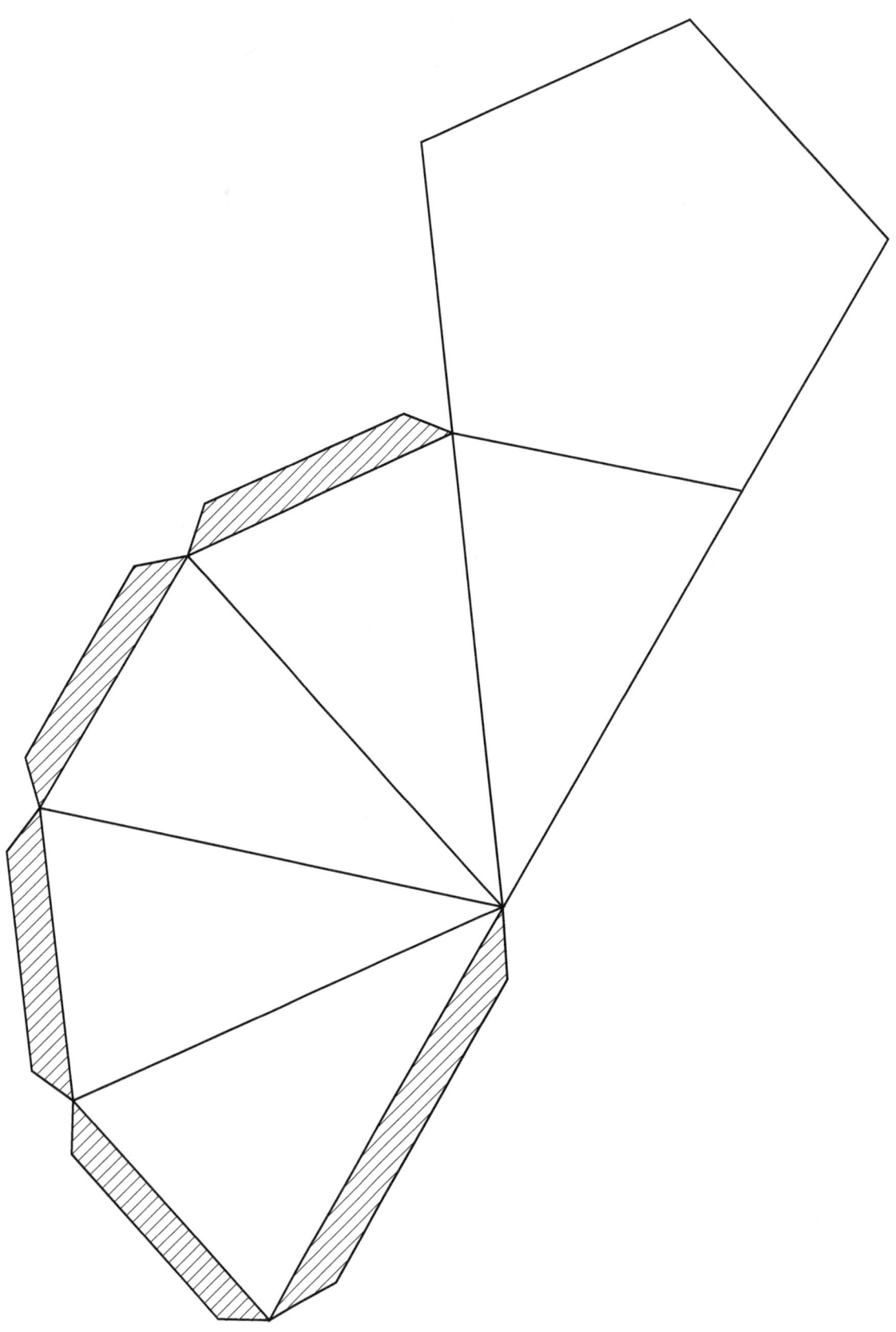

Figure 17 Pentagon Pyramid
From *Mathematics in the K–8 Classroom and Library* by Sueanne McKinney and KaaVonia Hinton. Santa Barbara, CA: Linworth. Copyright © 2010.

Title Index

A

About Time: A First Look at Time and Clocks, 82–83
Action of Subtraction, 39
Actual Size, 82
Adventures of Penrose the Mathematical Cat, 54–55
Alexander, Who Used to Be Rich Last Sunday, 80
All of the Above: A Novel, 73
Amanda Bean's Amazing Dream, 27–29
Anno's Magic Seeds, 38–39
Apple Fractions, 47
Arctic Fives Arrive, 47–48

B

Beetle McGrady Eats Bugs, 98–100
Best of Times, 22
Big Numbers: And Pictures That Show Just How Big They Are!, 47
Bunny Money, 85

C

Can You Count to a Googol?, 50
Cat in Numberland, 40–41
Centipede's 100 Shoes, 36–37
Cheetah Math: Learning about Division from Baby Cheetahs, 46
Chicken Soup, 102
Chimp Math: Learning about Time from a Baby Chimpanzee, 83
City by Numbers, 66
Cloak for the Dreamer, 71
Clocks and More Clocks, 78–79
Cloudy with a Chance of Meatballs, 88–89
Cool Cats Counting, 49
Creepy Countdown, 3, 16
Cubes, Cones, Cylinders and Spheres, 71
Cut and Assemble 3-D Geometric Shapes: Ten Models in Full Color, 74

D

Daisy 1, 2, 3, 39
Dealing with Addition, 44
Diary of a Worm, 103
Doorbell Rang, 35–36
Do the Math: Secrets, Lies, and Algebra, 58–59
Do You Wanna Bet?, 93–94
Draw Me a Star, 66–67
Dreaming: A Countdown to Sleep, 17
Duck Dunks, 39

E

Each Orange Had 8 Slices: A Counting Book, 42
Eating Fractions, 45
Estela's Swap, 106
Euclid: The Great Geometer, 71

F

Fellowship of the Ring, 11
Fish, Swish! Splash, Dash!: Counting Round and Round, 44
Fish Eyes: A Book You Can Count On, 17
Follow the Money!, 83
Fractals, Googles and other Mathematical Tales, 57
Fraction Action, 44
Fraction Fun, 38
Full House: An Invitation to Fractions, 33–34
Fun with Roman Numerals, 38

G

Gathering: A Northwoods Counting Book, 39
Give Me Half, 45–46
Gobble-Gobble Crash: A Barnyard Counting Bash, 49
Going North, 103–104
Grandfather Tang's Story, 63–66
Grapes of Math, 21–22
Great Divide, 40
Great Estimations, 42
Great Graph Contest, 95
Great Number Rumble, 43
Greedy Triangle, 66

H

Have a Good Day Cafe, 106
Heads or Tails?: Exploring Probability through Games, 96
Hershey's Kisses Addition Book, 23
Hershey's Kisses Subtraction Book, 23
Hershey's Milk Chocolate Fraction Book, 3
Hershey's Milk Chocolate Weights and Measures, 84
Higher Geometry, 73
Hobbit, 11
Hoop Kings: Poems, 107
How Big Is It?: A BIG Book all about BIGNESS, 82
How Do You Know What Time It Is?, 85
How High Can a Dinosaur Count?: And Other Math Mysteries, 41
How Hungry Are You?, 46
How Many Bears?, 58
How Many Feet in the Bed?, 22
How Tall?: Facts, Records, and Height Comparisons of Ordinary and Extraordinary Things, 81–82
How Tall, How Short, How Faraway, 77–78
How the Arabs Invented Algebra: The History of the Concept of Variables, 58
How the Second Grade Got $8,205.50 to Visit the Statue of Liberty, 19

I

If America Were a Village, 91
If the World Were a Village, 90–91
Inchworm and a Half, 48
In My Backyard, 42
Is It Larger? Is It Smaller?, 82
It's Probably Penny, 95
I Spy Shapes in Art, 73
I Spy Two Eyes: Numbers in Art, 45

J

Jingle Dancer, 107
Jump, Kangaroo, Jump!, 45
Just Like Josh Gibson, 104

K

King's Chessboard, 51–53
King's Commissioners, 3, 41
Knick-knack Paddy Whack, 41

L

Lemonade for Sale, 92–93
Lemonade War, 81
Less Than Zero, 59
Let's Count, 42
Let's Count the Puppies, 43
Librarian Who Measured the Earth, 72
Look Whooo's Counting, 44–45
Lots and Lots of Zebra Stripes: Patterns in Nature, 74
Lunch Money, 81

M

M&M's Color Pattern Book, 72
M&M's Count to One Hundred Book, 17
Man Who Walked between the Towers, 103
Math Appeal, 22,
Math Curse, 3, 56–57
Mathematicles!, 4
Math Fables, 22
Math Fair Blues, 72
Math for All Seasons, 22
Math Potatoes, 22
Marvelous Math: A Book of Poems, 4
Me and the Measure of Things, 84–85
Measuring Penny, 83
Me Counting Time: From Seconds to Centuries, 84
Mighty Maddie, 83
Million Dots, 39
Millions to Measure, 79–80
Minnie's Diner: A Multiplying Menu, 3, 40
Missing Math: A Number Mystery, 44
Mission: Addition, 24
Money Madness, 81
Monster Who Did My Math, 48
Mummy Math: An Adventure in Geometry, 68
Museum Shapes, 72–73
My Rows and Piles of Coins, 83

N

Napping House, 22
Neil's Numberless World, 3, 18
Number Devil: A Mathematical Adventure, 53–54

O

Ocean Counting: Odd Numbers, 47
Olivia . . . and the Missing Toy, 100–101
On Beyond a Million: An Amazing Math Journey, 48
One, Two, Three, Go!, 44
One Boy, 48
One Hundred Hungry Ants, 24–26
One Less Fish, 17
One Odd Day, 41
One Riddle, One Answer, 49
On Time: From Seasons to Split Seconds, 84

P

Perfect Snowman, 97–98
Pickles to Pittsburgh, 89
Piece = Part = Portion, 34–35
Pigs at Odds: Fun with Math and Games, 95
Pigs Go to the Market: Halloween Fun with Math and Shopping, 31
Pizza Counting, 39–40
Polar Bear Math: Learning about Fractions from Klondike and Snow, 46
Probably Pistachio, 95–96

R

Real Princess: A Mathemagical Tale, 50
Remainder of One, 29–30
Roar: A Noisy Counting Book, 40

S

Sea Shapes, 72
Sea Sums, 43
Second Is a Hiccup: A Child's Book of Time, 82
7 × 9 = Trouble!, 68
Shanghai Messenger, 103
Shape of Things, 70
Shape Up!: Fun with Triangles and Other Polygons, 70
Show Way, 107–108
Sir Cumference and the Dragon of Pi, 62
Sir Cumference and the First Round Table, 4, 62–63
Sir Cumference and the Great Night of Angleland, 62
Sir Cumference and the Isle of Immeter, 62
Sir Cumference and the Sword in the Cone, 62
Sky Boys: How They Built the Empire State Building, 104
So Many Circles, So Many Squares, 71
Spaghetti and Meatballs for All!, 31–32
Star in My Orange: Looking for Nature's Shapes, 73–74
String of Beads, 106–107
Subtraction Action, 23–24
Swamp Angel, 101
Sweet Potato Pie, 105

T

Telling Time: How to Tell Time on Digital and Analog Clocks!, 83–84
Ten, Nine, Eight, 39
Ten Red Apples, 43
Ten Tiny Tickles, 43
Thirteen Moons on a Turtle's Back: A Native American Year of Moons, 102–103
Those Building Men, 104
365 Penguins, 41–42
Tiger Math: Learning to Graph from a Baby Tiger, 96
Token Gift, 59
Tools of Timekeeping: A Kid's Guide to the History and Science of Telling Time, 81
Top Secret: A Handbook of Codes, Ciphers, and Secret Writing, 58
Triangle for Adaora: An African Book of Shapes, 73
Tricking the Tallyman, 89–90
Twelve Snails to One Lizard: A Tale of Mischief and Measurement, 3, 76–77
Twenty Is Too Many, 40
Twizzlers: Shapes and Patterns, 73

Two at the Zoo: A Counting Book, 49
Two of Everything: A Chinese Folktale, 42–43
Two Short, Two Long: A Book about Rectangles, 71–72
2 × 2 = Boo, 30–31

U

Underwater Counting: Even Numbers, 47
Uno's Garden, 39

V

Very Improbable Story: A Math Adventure, 95

W

What's a Pair? What's a Dozen?, 49
What's Faster Than a Speeding Cheetah?, 85
What's Your Angle, Pythagoras?: A Math Adventure, 70–71
When a Line Bends . . . A Shape Begins, 71
Where We Play Sports: Measuring the Perimeters of Polygons, 74
Who Made This Cake?, 106
Who's Got Spots?, 94
Wishing Club, 32–33
Wombat Walkabout, 49
Working with Fractions, 38

Y

You Can't Buy a Dinosaur with a Dime: Problem Solving in Dollars and Cents, 85
Your 206 Bones, 32 Teeth, and Other Body Math, 46

Z

Zachary Zormer Shape Transformer: A Math Adventure, 74

Author Index

A

Aber, Linda Williams, 94
Adams, Colleen, 5
Adler, David, 38, 56, 69, 70, 77, 81
American Association of School Librarians, 9
Anno, Mitsumasa, 38, 52–53, 69
Axelrod, Amy, 31, 95

B

Baker, Keith, 4
Ball, Johnny, 52
Bang, Molly, 39
Barrett, Judi, 88
Base, Graeme, 39
Bernstein, Allison T., 11
Berry, Lynne, 39
Bezuk, Nadine, 16, 19, 20, 24–25, 32, 61–62, 75, 87
Bickel, Cindy, 46, 83
Birch, David, 51
Bloom, Valerie, 4
Blum, Raymond, 52
Bowen, Betsy, 39
Brown, Margaret Wise, 19
Bruchac, Joseph, 102
Burns, Marilyn, 2, 31, 56, 66, 69

C

Capraro, Mary, 2
Capraro, Robert Michael, 2
Carle, Eric, 66–67
Catalanotto, Peter, 39
Cathcart, W. George, 16, 19, 20, 24–25, 32, 61–62, 75, 87
Cheng, Andrea, 103
Child, Lauren, 19
Cleary, Brian P., 39
Clements, Andrew, 39, 81
Coats, Lucy, 3, 18
Cooper, J. David, 4
Cronin, Doreen, 103
Cushman, Jean, 93

D

Davies, Jacqueline, 81, 89
Dickinson, Gail K., 9
Dobson, Christina, 39
Dodds, Dayle Ann, 3, 33, 40, 69–70
Doll, Carol, 12
Downey, Tika, 58
Duke, Kate, 19, 40

E

Edens, Cooper, 58
Edwards, Pamela Duncan, 40
Ehlert, Lois, 17, 69
Einhorn, Edward, 95
Ekeland, Ivar, 40
Ellis, Julie, 70
Engels, Christiane, 41
Enzensberger, Han Magnus, 53
Ezell, Michelle, 2

F

Falconer, Ian, 100
Farmer, Lesley S. J., 9, 12
Finch, Katherine, 9
Fisher, Doris, 41
Fisher, Valorie, 41
Flemming, Dan, 10–11
Formichelli, Linda, 81
Franco, Betsy, 4
Friedman, Aileen, 3, 41, 71
Fromental, Jean-Luc, 41

G

Gardner, Judy, 9–10
Gerstein, Mordicai, 103
Gifford, Scott, 34
Giganti, Paul, 42
Giogas, Valarie, 42
Goldstone, Bruce, 42
Greene, Rhonda Gowler, 71
Greenstein, Elaine, 17

H

Halsey, Pamela, 2
Hamilton-Pennell, Christine, 10
Hamm, Diane Johnston, 22
Harrington, Janice N., 103
Harris, Nicholas, 81
Hayhurst, Chris, 71
Hellwig, Stacey, 2, 12
Hiebert, James, 1
Hightower, Susan, 3, 76
Hillman, Ben, 82
Hinton, KaaVonia, 9
Hoban, Tana, 42, 69, 71, 82
Holub, Joan, 56
Hong, Lily Toy, 42
Hopkins, Lee Bennett, 4
Hopkinson, Deborah, 104
Huck, Charlotte, 3, 16
Hulme, Joy N., 43
Hunsader, Patricia, 2
Hutchins, Hazel, 82
Hutchins, Pat, 35, 43, 78

I

Isaacs, Anne, 101

J

Jacobs, Jim, 2, 12
Janeczko, Paul B., 58
Jenkins, Steve, 82
Johnson, Angela, 104
Johnson, Stephen T., 43
Jones, Christianne C., 71

K

Kassirer, Sue, 72
Katz, Karen, 43
Kiger, Nancy, 4
King, Andrew, 52
Koller, Jackie French, 19
Koscielniak, Bruce, 82
Kunhardt, Katharine, 43

L

Lance, Keith Curry, 10
Lasky, Kathryn, 72
Lee, Cora, 43
Lee, Huy Voun, 44
Leedy, Lorren, 23–24, 30, 44, 69, 83, 95
Lewis, J. Patrick, 56
Lichtman, Wendy, 58
Lindsey, Kathleen D., 105
Livingston, Nancy, 2
London, Jonathan, 102
Long, Lynette, 5, 44, 52

M

MacDonald, Suse, 44, 72
Maganzini, Christy, 52
Mannis, Celeste Davidson, 4
Martin, Jannelle, 56
Martin, W. Eric, 81
McDaniels, Preston, 97
McDonald, Megan, 98
McGrath, Barbara Barbieri, 17, 56, 69, 72
McKellar, Danica, 52
McKibbon, Hugh William, 59
McMillan, Bruce, 45, 69
Merriam, Eve, 19
Metropolitan Museum of Art, 72
Michelson, Richard, 4
Micklethwait, Lucy, 45, 73
Mills, Claudia, 45
Minkel, Walter, 10–11
Mollel, Tololwa M., 83
Monroe, Eula, 2, 12
Moranville, Sharelle Byars, 73
Murphy, Stuart J., 45, 59, 69, 83, 92, 95

N

Nagda, Ann Whitehead, 46, 83, 96
Nakagawa, Chihiro, 106
Napoli, Donna Jo, 32, 46
Napoli, Mary, 2
National Council of Teachers of Mathematics, 2–3, 5, 10, 15–16, 51, 61–62, 75–76, 87–88, 92
Neuschwander, Cindy, 4, 27, 29, 62, 68–69

O

O'Keefe, Susan Heyboer, 19
Older, Jules, 83
O'Neill, Alexis, 106
Onyefulu, Ifeoma, 73
O'Reilly, Gillian, 43
O'Sullivan, Robyn, 46

P

Packard, Edward, 47
Pallotta, Jerry, 3, 19, 23, 47, 69, 73, 84
Pappas, Theoni, 52, 54, 57
Park, Frances, 106
Park, Ginger, 106
Pearsall, Shelley, 73
Pinczes, Elinor J., 24, 28, 47, 69
Pothier, Yvonne, 16, 19–20, 24–25, 32, 61–62, 75, 87

R

Ransome, James E., 104
Rau, Dana Meachen, 73
Reid, H., 18
Reid, Margarette S., 106
Reisberg, Joanne A., 74
Rose, Deborah Lee, 4
Ross, Tony, 36
Roza, Greg, 74, 96
Ryan, Pam Muñoz, 19

S

Schiro, Michael, 2
Schnitzlein, Danny, 48
Schomberg, Janie, 9
Schwartz, David M., 48, 69, 79
Scieszka, Jon, 3, 56
Seeger, Laura, 48
Shahan, Sherry, 49
Sheffield, Stephanie, 2
Sheldrick Ross, Catherine, 52
Shields, Carol Diggory, 49
Shivertaker, Jill, 2, 9
Skurzynski, Gloria, 84

Small, Ruth, 9
Smith, Albert G., 74
Smith, Charles R., 107
Smith, Cynthia Leitich, 107
Smith, Danna, 49
Smith, David J., 90–91
Smith, Lane, 56
Sweeney, Joan, 84
Swinburne, Stephen R., 49, 74

T

Tang, Greg, 21–22, 56, 69
Tchen, Richard, 46
Thompson, Lauren, 49
Toft, Kim Michelle, 17
Tolkien, J.R.R., 11
Tompert, Ann, 63

V

Vance, James, 16, 19–20, 24–25, 32, 61–62, 75, 87
VanCleave, Janice Pratt, 52
Van De Walle, John, 3–4, 15–17, 19, 24–25, 61–62, 75
Van Leeuwen, Jean, 102
Viorst, Judith, 80

W

Wallace, Faith, 2, 9
Ward, Robin, 2
Welborn, Lynda, 10
Welch, Wayne, 1
Wells, Robert E., 50, 69, 85
Wells, Rosemary, 85
Whitin, David, 2
Whitin, Phyllis, 2
Wilburne, Jane, 2
Wilde, Sandra, 2
Williams, Brenda, 50
Wingard-Nelson, Rebecca, 5
Winter, Jeanette, 19
Wise, William, 19
Wolk-Stanley, Jessica, 5
Woods, Audrey, 22

Woodson, Jacqueline, 107
Wyatt, Valerie, 52

Y

Yolen, Jane, 4

Z

Zaslavsky, Claudia, 52
Ziefert, Harriet, 85
Zimelman, Nathan, 19